Finding Cynthia Winters

Finding Cynthia Winters

Sue Watson

LASAVIA
PUBLISHING

Published by Lasavia Publishing,
Auckland, New Zealand
www.lasaviapublishing.com

ISBN: 978-1-991083-43-2

Contents

DEDICATION

This is for my son Max.

This is for the birth mothers who couldn't hold their babies.

This is for the birth fathers who never knew.

This is for the grandparents who never knew or did know, but were ashamed.

This is for the sisters and brothers of the birth mothers who knew and
had to keep the secret.

This is for the caregivers who helped at the birth and cared for the babies.

This is for the adoptive parents who were given a baby and tried to be
the best parents they could be.

This is for the aunties and uncles and cousins of the adopted baby who
knew and welcomed the baby into their family.

This is for the adopted babies who were born in secret and shame,

The babies lied about and the babies hidden,

The babies who were nameless and cared for by strangers,

The babies who were given a new name in a new family,

Who could not know the mother and father from whom they came.

Collecting Fragments

It's early Saturday morning and I'm tucked up in bed with my blue wooden tea tray, my teapot with the red knitted tea cosy, my tea strainer and my Belle Fiore painted china teacup and saucer. This is my safe place, and the tears are here as I think of my only child, Max, and the story I want to tell him. How I long to break the silence. Yet, how much I struggle when I'm with him, my most important relationship, the only person in my life who has my blood and my DNA. Maybe knowing this put too much of a burden on him. So let me try and begin to tell this story, so that the truth can finally be told.

I close my eyes. My own kind of prayer, this telling. I am safe here in my bed. It is time to be courageous, to go on this journey, because the story must be told.

In my hands is a beautiful round river stone. Not a boulder, but large enough to need both hands to lift. Starting is about first becoming familiar with the stone. I take my time to feel it, to rub my palms slowly over its curves, the small cracks, the indentations. I know the coolness of the stone in the morning and the warmth of the stone at night as it slowly releases its heat. This morning the stone is cold.

These river stones are common to the farms and paddocks of Aotearoa. Upriver, they begin their rolling journey down the mountains. Some break along the way, becoming smaller and smoother against the tumble of the water, until they end up spread across the river flats.

This story has become a collection of stones. Fragmented over time, chips lost along the way. A letter received, a phone call, a bedside conversation at a hospice building, a glimpse of a brother I have never known through a glass door.

My work, my telling of this story, is to walk about the field and gather up the stones. Some lie exposed and easy to find. Others hide under soil and grass; lichen and moss have tried to claim them. Now, it's time to kneel down on the earth and begin to rub away the soil that time has made.

This is a story I've tried to tell before but I always stopped myself and let the stream of life's force claim me. There would come a time, I knew, when it would be the right moment to sit down and start. To simply pick up the cold stone, run my hands across its grainy surface, and begin to turn it gently, to slowly warm it with the heat of my hands and my body and wait for the sun to rise.

In my mind, a woman walks into a pond, the banks lined with reeds. She has filled the pockets of her dress with stones, and holds a stone gripped in each of her hands. Her eyes look forward across the water and her feet step slowly and deliberately, deeper and deeper until the water rises to her waist, then to her chest and neck. Without flinching, she steps again and the water rises above her head until she has disappeared. Only small bubbles and a widening ripple is left.

The stones of this story weigh me down. If I don't release them, they will pull me deeper into the water. They will hasten my death. One stone on its own isn't so heavy. It can be tossed and caught and carried in a pocket unnoticed. One stone doesn't feel like a burden, but this story is an entire river of them. I am stronger now, strong enough to carry them all, but it is time to put them down. For myself, for Max, for all those who have traversed this path of facing their truth.

Introduction

Opening the Box

'Tell the truth, tell the truth, tell the truth.'
Sheryl Louise Moller

Today begins The Lizzy Project, the story of my birth mother. It is my responsibility to record, so that this history will not die with me. I am the only person left with all its fragments, and the only one interested in putting them back together. It is a story about me, and the people who share my blood – but it is also about what it means to be erased.

My work begins alone in a room at the Quaker's 'Friends House' on Waiheke Island. At the centre of a long wooden trestle table is a white cardboard box. I sit down, close my eyes, and place my hands gently on the box.

Inside are journal entries, notebooks, and letters that span nearly forty years, a collection I have put to the side for a time I knew would eventually come. Some envelopes have official stamps marking their legitimacy; others have past addresses of mine handwritten below my name. My first task is to lay them out, to touch them and see them, to allow myself to feel their powerful resonance. These fragments contain a life force; it is my job to make them whole again. It is now time to open the box.

I put them in chronological order as best I can. The earliest letter is in a brown envelope stamped O.H.M.S, dated 16 February 1987. On the other end of the table, the last of my collection is an envelope with the 'Blue Lizzy Museum Collection' logo in the bottom left-hand corner. Inside is the last letter I received from her, my birth mother. It is postmarked

February 2005, a month after her death. It was sent to me fifteen years ago by her lawyer. Now, I am approaching my sixtieth birthday, nearing the age that Lizzy herself passed away.

I count the letters – twenty six. Some of them I haven't read since I received them. How will I approach this enormous task? I hope they will make more sense now, that the distance from them will give me a clearer perspective, unshackled from the emotional load. Some memories float to the surface with surprising clarity, but others I can hardly recall. For those, I must rely on the clues from these letters to tell the story.

It is time to try. It is time to follow these unworn paths I began long ago, and search again for the truths I know are here. Thus begins my work of uncovering my history and asking the questions that have simmered under the surface for years. Who was my birth mother, Lizzy, and why did she leave me with so many half-told stories? Why are her children, my supposed half-sister and half-brother, so determined to keep me at a distance? Which of the two men Lizzy described is actually my birth father? And most importantly, if I find these answers, what will I learn about myself?

CHAPTER ONE

The Lamb White Days

'Nothing I cared, in the lamb white days, that time would take me
Up to the swallow thronged loft by the shadow of my hand,
In the moon this is always rising'

'Fern Hill,' Dylan Thomas

I always knew I was adopted. There was no fiction attempted about where I had come from, and I was never made to feel anything less than a true member of my large and loving extended family. On the twelfth of November, 1962, at two weeks old, I was placed into the care of Cicely and Peter Watson, my Mum and Dad. They brought me home, introduced me to my sister Wendy, eighteen months older and also adopted as a baby, and I began my new life.

I was celebrated and instantly loved by Mum and Dad. But I wasn't exactly like other babies. I couldn't suck or take a bottle. Mum had to hold me firmly in the crook of her arm, sitting at the table with a cup of warm formula and a teaspoon. With one hand she would prise my mouth open like the beak of a tiny bird, and with the other, spoon feed the milk into my mouth. How laborious and time-consuming that must have been. I wonder if she was disappointed and scared thinking that she had been given a baby who was broken in some way, a baby that refused.

Of course, this makes sense now. How would I have learned to suckle if I had been separated from my mother at birth? I guess most of the other babies lined up for adoption in the nursery would've taken a bottle, as there's no way the nurses could have spoon fed more than one or two of them. Did I take a bottle in the hospital, but then refuse on arrival at Mum and Dad's? I don't know. I never thought to ask Mum, and it is too late now.

I don't doubt that at times Mum must have been frustrated and exhausted with her two babies under the age of two, one who took hours to feed. If she was, though, she never let on this frustration to us. Knowing Mum, her determination to be the best mother would have overwritten her fear, and she would have set about in her farmer's daughter depression-era way of making the most of a difficult situation.

I still have a green Irish dinner plate of Mum's that she inherited from her mother. At some stage it broke in half, and the years had browned and hardened the epoxy glue at the edges of the crack. Mum was always doing this, always intent on repairing the damage. She had taken the two halves of the broken plate and did her best to make it whole again. It didn't matter that you could still see the break – it was still a plate worth keeping, cherishing, loving. And it was in this way Mum set about gluing her broken little girl back together.

I have photos of me as a baby lying on a chequered woollen blanket on the lawn. One with Wendy kneeling and smiling, and me lying back in Mum's arms. I was on display in a white baby gown. Mum dark-haired in her summer frock, smiling and beautiful, and me frowning.

Is it an exaggeration to say there are no photos of me as a baby smiling? I don't think so. I've gone back through the albums I have from Mum and Dad and I couldn't find any. I was a baby who frowned, who looked out at the world with a worried gaze. Even Mum's loving determination to fix me and her constant smile was not enough to undo my frown.

I remember as a younger woman I would be admonished to smile. I would stop and realise I was frowning at the world, pissed off that as a woman I was expected to go about with a smile on my face. You can see the frown marks now deeply marked in my forehead and between my eyebrows. I don't consciously notice them, but still in meetings sometimes, someone will pause and look across at me and say, 'Is everything all right? Are you OK?' and I realise that once again I've reverted to frowning concentration.

There are some things I will never know. One of them is where I learned to frown. Maybe I took on this tendency in my early years of adjustment, recovering from those handful of motherless days. Maybe it was etched into my DNA, a scar of trauma passed down from generation to generation.

Growing up, my 'difficult' personality was often ascribed to my dad, Peter. Mum always said that the reason Dad and I fought so often was because we were so alike. 'Oh,' she'd say, 'You're so like your father.' And it seemed true. We both had a short fuse, we were both driven, and both wanted the world to fit us better. Without a doubt, nurture plays a big part in how we form and grow and interact with the world, but I've come to realise and believe that these traits are written upon the natural material with which we are born. How we are raised, as far as I have seen, is simply an expression of our predetermined genes.

My intense behavioural abnormalities got to the point that Mum took me to see a child psychologist when I was still quite young, which would have been virtually unheard of in the early 1960s. At some point, my unpredictable tantrums far surpassed my dad's supposedly passed-down short fuse.

There have been so many fractures along the way. Yet, most days, my Mum seemed so grateful, so joyful simply to have her chance to be a mother. To do the best for 'her girls'. Adoption was something Wendy and I wore like a badge of honour. It made us special and unique. We were *chosen*. From the moment we entered their lives, Mum and Dad did everything they possibly could to give us a good home and a loving childhood.

Our little world on the quarter acre section in Te Atatu in West Auckland was, in hindsight, the kind of ideal childhood that I now know many of my friends and family weren't lucky enough to experience.

We were a tight, 'normal' little Anglican family of four. Being just west of Auckland, we had all the amenities that a city could offer – Brownies, gymnastics, drama club, swimming – without missing out on the freedom of a Kiwi country life – horse riding lessons and a pet lamb who would arrive each year to graze the lawn and then go to another 'happy place' on its first birthday. Even during tough financial times, our parents always made us the priority.

Our house was *the* house. Dad dug us a swimming pool by hand in the back garden, and it became a favourite spot for our teenage friends through high school. Mum was kind and patient and endlessly supportive. I'll never forget the feeling of coming home from school, the smell of warm Afghan biscuits wafting to greet me up the driveway. Mum, waiting there, excited to ask us about our day.

So, when people asked me what I thought of being adopted, I told them quite blankly and truthfully – 'I don't.' My birth mother, who I assumed must exist somewhere, hardly crossed my mind. She was a blank void behind me, irrelevant to all the opportunity and love and life that had opened in front of me after my adoption. What mattered growing up was the family I knew – my sister Wendy, my dad Peter, my mum Cicely, and my large bunch of cousins, aunties and uncles.

It was what you could call a perfect adoption, the kind advertised by government agencies. I was wiped clean, returned to factory settings. You're supposed to be able to start from scratch when you adopt a baby. Adoptive parents are promised a *tabula rasa*, a blank canvas to fill up with all the love and history of their own selves, values and whakapapa.

But history never really leaves us. We know that history matters, even if it shakes our sense of self. Especially if it shakes our sense of self. While our memories and our stories might be erased, there are some things that are never perfectly wiped clean as we're told they can be.

I was never told the reason why I was adopted. I think we were given a standard story that went something like, 'Your mother loved you but wasn't able to look after you.' But lurking in the background were other more sinister possibilities. Perhaps she didn't love me, or want me. Or worse, she was the victim of rape, a victim of incest (God forbid), or she was mentally unwell and I was forcibly removed from her.

Then came a flood of changes with the Adult Adoption Information Act in 1985. There had been plenty of stories in the media about how the new adoption laws were allowing birth mothers to seek out their long lost children. Birth parents and adopted children could apply through the State to be put in touch with one another. But both parties had to agree to release their name and address. If they refused, that's where the road would end.

I was in my mid-twenties at the time. Since my late teens, I had been living in Wellington – first working and then studying at Victoria University. After a 'born-again' experience, I became deeply entrenched with the Charismatic Christian movement, where I met my ex-husband, Jono.

In those years, I had a sense that my birth mother was likely still out there, but I certainly didn't have any inclination to take up the opportunity from the law change. It was at this stage in my life, age twenty-four, living in a flat in Newtown when I received a small, fat, brown envelope with the Department of Social Welfare letterhead.

CHAPTER TWO

The First Letter

I knew as soon as I saw the envelope. My birth mother was knocking on the door. The unopened letter felt heavy and significant in my hand, a sense of portent washed through me. There would be no going back. Once I read its contents, I would not be able to forget them.

16 February 1987
With the compliments of The Department of Social Welfare

How odd and inappropriate this language seemed. When handling the lives, the identities and secrets of people, the language of the state put forward a wrong-footed formality. In those first words, written as though I was being invited to a dinner party, I received my first glimpse into my world before being adopted.

Inside were two handwritten letters:

C/- Student Mail
Massey University

16.02.87

Dear Sir/Madam,

Reference S 8-11. Re Adoption Information.

First and foremost — well done! I have received your advice regarding your success with your search for my daughter & I thank you most sincerely.

However, to business.

I confirm that I wish you to proceed with the inquiry, I would like total contact but I am also prepared to accept whatever level or depth of contact that my daughter may wish. Yes, you may pass on my present name & address to my daughter. I have included some brief information about myself for my daughter & assume that you will cull or censor what you feel is not appropriate to pass on at this early stage. I have attached separately.

Finally, may I thank you once again, please accept my sincere gratitude.

Yours sincerely,

Lizzy
(Elizabeth J Mackenzie née: Winters)

The second letter in the envelope had no greeting. It read:

I am known as Lizzy (short for Elizabeth), I am 45 years of age currently engaged in a programme of tertiary education. I shortly commenced my second year of an MA in Psychology. I also work for the University as a supervisor of a student hostel. I was married for 20 years, and have 2 other children by that marriage, & am now separated. To help provide a mental picture of myself, I am a 5' 5" tall, medium weight – a typical middle-aged woman with shoulder length hair and glasses.

Well that brief resume I hope provides some of the basic nut & bolt type of information. I would also like to add that I have waited 24 years to see and know my daughter and can wait a little longer if need be; that is whatever is right & OK for her is OK for me if she feels she would like more time or preparation.

My other message is simply this – I love her & I have always loved her. You may or may not pass that on as you wish.

In just two small pages of text, I had learned more about my life before Mum and Dad than I had in the rest of my twenty-four years.

A glimpse of a woman's life – my birth mother's life – came into view. I calculated that she was twenty years old when she gave me up for adoption, older than I had expected. I had always assumed she was a teenager, too young to raise a child on her own.

After she gave birth to me, she married and had two more children, my half-siblings I assumed. I tried to picture them, to picture her, a 'typical middle-aged woman,' shorter than me, with a need for glasses.

She was separated from her husband, living and working at a student hostel, and studying a Masters in Psychology when she began her search for me. So she was an academic. Though I was only at the beginning of my own studies when I got the letter, I would later go on to complete a doctorate at Victoria University and also spend two years supervising an international student hostel. I too would eventually separate from my husband.

At once, I felt conflicting reactions all competing for space in my mind. Curiosity about my birth mother, for the first time I can ever remember, had presented itself to me. But alongside that curiosity there was also a strong sense of discomfort and fear. What did this woman want from me? I had my family, and all the love I needed. I had no intention of building a new connection, a potentially painful connection, simply because we shared blood.

My whole life until that point had been built on the pretence that I could nullify my existence before Mum and Dad. I was chosen by them – and therefore, I must have been *unchosen* by my birth mother. This letter, an extension of a phantom hand into my carefully re-born life, was asking me to see it all differently. To go from ignoring this previous existence to embracing it.

But then, I imagined her writing this letter, waiting all these years. A sense of compassion, almost pity, grew in me. To completely ignore that pain and the strength it would have taken Lizzy to draft these words felt cruel. If I had the power to give this woman some kind of closure, then didn't I owe her that?

The next day, I replied to the letter, giving her my name and postal address.

The year of 1987 passed quickly. I was preparing my wedding, consumed with all the day-to-day busyness of work, study, and church. Even now, I can hardly remember what I wrote back to Lizzy. She was still, at that time, altogether separate from my life.

I had no idea how quickly that separation would dissolve, then harden, dissolve again, and become a familiar rip and repair over the next twenty years. Sitting here now, decades later, looking at the yellowed pages, slowly smoothing my hand over the folds of these boxed up letters, I ask that distracted, twenty-five-year-old new bride what she remembers.

I was married in December that year, and Jono and I moved in together into a flat in Newtown. Just a few months later, I received a letter of congratulations from Lizzy. The card shows a painting of old-fashioned blue irises on the front – the rich sweet-scented ones that Mum used to grow.

> *To Sue and Jonathan,*
>
> *A very late celebration of a wedding. Congratulations and I wish you both the very best for the future.*
>
> *My love,*
> *Lizzy*

Along with the card came an original print that I still have of Kāpiti Island signed by Malcolm Wall. No doubt it was a view similar to the one from the home she lived in while married and raising her family in Paekākāriki,

Wellington, something she told me in one of our later conversations.

I'm not sure how long I took to reply to her first letter, and don't remember what it said. It must have been a while, as the next letter from Lizzy in my box of history arrived in September. Lizzy's address changed; she was still living in Palmerston North, but had moved out of the student hostel.

When I opened the envelope, an oddly-shaped photo no larger than a finger slid out from the folded sheets of paper. It was a full body image of Lizzy, and it appeared she had taken a pair of scissors to a larger photo, presumably filled with other posing figures.

I could see myself in the tiny face looking questioningly back at me. There were my cheeks with an extra twenty years of life on them, pulled into a distorted expression as though she were chewing on a piece of food. It was hardly a flattering photo, but she looked slender and fashionable in a white dress and seated with her legs crossed. I noticed the shape of her calves, immediately recognising them as my own. I had always considered my legs to be my best feature, and I could see in an instant where I had inherited them.

Before I had even opened her letter, my entire body had gone rigid as though a wash of cold water had blown through me. There she was. Unsmiling. Cut out from the rest of the world. Cut away from whatever context warranted this photo, or the people who had accompanied her on the day. I recognised what this unnaturally isolated photo communicated: *those people have no place in these letters. This correspondence is just me and you.* With the chill of the photo still in my bones, and her mid-chew expression still in my mind, I turned to the enclosed letter.

09.09.88

Dear Sue,

Thank you, both for your letter and the photo. You do not have to apologise for the time taken to contact me; you had time. It was enough for me last year to know that you were available and I was happy to wait until such time as you felt ready.

Also Sue I would like to thank you for mentioning your parents. I had thought long and hard about how contact may affect them, your relationship with them, plus yourself but my wish/desire to look after all your best interests was overridden by my need to know that you were actually alive and well.

I also wanted you to know that there was someone else available for you within your wider family network.

To a literary/literature ? (how does one say that!) woman that you are, I can say, 'My cup runneth over!' My basic needs have been met – more than I expected in that the details you shared of yourself and the photo are a bonus.

There is no way that I will interfere in your life. What you need and want are my prime concerns and I am happy to respond to anything you wish or may request.

My apologies in that this reply is delayed but I have moved from Massey and only received your letter today. I am now flatting at the above address while I finish off my Diploma – hopefully at the end of the year. What I shall do then is anybody's guess but knowing me some brilliant (or as others say, some crazy!) idea will surface.

I can only vaguely remember the details that I put in my first letter, but you know that I have ghastly handwriting, am a rotten speller and my English ain't too hot either! So be it. I have enclosed a photo of myself, I must say it flatters me, it was taken last year, but it will give you some idea – I am the one in white.

Sue, thank you for taking your time. That says a lot to me about you as a person. I am happy to have further contact with you. Whatever you choose and whatever pace you wish.

My love,
Lizzy (Mackenzie)

It surprised me to hear her describe the photo as flattering. Her face wasn't smiling or posed at all. It made her look vulnerable, caught off guard, thin.

Putting these thoughts aside as I finished the letter, I considered that final promise – *whatever you choose*. She had batted the ball back to me, allowing me the control of when and what to do next. Yet, it seemed late for this kind of promise. We had already come so far, divulged so much. It was impossible to backtrack. I must have replied to this, probably thanking her again, and though I cannot remember clearly, the next letter in my box suggests it was me who asked to meet in person.

24.11.88

Dear Sue,

Thank you for your great letter. Yes I would love to meet you. Let me know which day would suit and I'll be there.

I've taken a little while to reply to the letter as with my last one, I was so excited and then went to bed realising that I could have written about another 100 pages and wishing that I had written lots of other things. I promise not to get that carried away but I would like to say that you sound like a rather fabulous individual. Together, you and your parents seem to have nurtured and developed an intelligent and talented woman not afraid to take risks and try other paths if the first seems less than satisfactory. That takes courage and tenacity which I think are rather special qualities and I feel that the former may help you through this new experience with me which may be not only strange but sometimes scary..

I admit to the latter, perhaps another reason for a slow reply – suddenly it seems as though I'm close to being put on the line and I'm a little scared that I won't be able to meet some of your preconceptions or images you may have built up of me. However I imagine that it will be only one of a number of emotions that I will experience (Yes! I read 'Reunions' too!). You mentioned that one experience may be for me to see my baby daughter grown; I have to admit that I had mentally aged you over the years – perhaps using my other daughter Julie as a marker, but I know when I saw your photo there was little surprise, except I had to readjust my image of you in that I had made you taller and older. Perhaps I needed to develop these images over time as it was a way for me to take you along with me through my separate life.

I think it's also important in this letter to mention two vivid memories that I have in my mind of you – one at birth and the other a week later. I was young and fit when you were born and you came very quickly, the midwife caught you and I instinctively sat up with my arms up to hold you when she said, 'You're not allowed to touch her.'

I remember feeling as if someone had chopped my arms off and it has taken me many years to come to terms with that. However I was a resilient individual and when I was to leave the hospital I demanded to see you – one to check you had OK eyes (mine are slightly mutated green & brown) 5 fingers and 5 toes etc and the other reason some confirmation that in fact you would be adopted.

I must admit they were good and coped with an uppity rebellious young woman and they let me look at you and the fact that you looked normal (and lovely) reassured me that there was no reason why you would not be adopted and allowed me to believe their verbal confirmation that in fact you were already an addition to a family.

So to go back to needs and wants, I think I mentioned in my last letter my need to know that you were alive and well, now that has been satisfied I can get into wants which may or may not be satisfied but one of my wishes is simply to hold you – not only for me to get a sense of completion for myself but perhaps in some way to make up to you a less than satisfactory beginning to your life.

Well that's enough of the emotional stuff but I think it's important to be honest with you and tell you where I am coming from, to do otherwise I feel would be less than worthy of you and our past relationship.

The other thing I wanted to mention (I promise the last!) was congratulations to you and Jonathan on your marriage.

I wish you and him the very best and I hope you will both be happy. Well done.
I look forward to hearing from you times and dates.

My love,
Lizzy

Now, reading these words of a woman now long gone, I find myself flinching. There is an immeasurable sense of unmet need, a desperation that still lurks behind the sentences all these years later.

It invokes in me a kind of horror reunion, a want for impossible repair. There I was, content, my life safe and protected, and there was Lizzy who ventured to find 'a sense of completion' with a single embrace. The gravity of her need had been frightening to me, and I felt my guard go up. My instinct was to protect myself against the enormity of it all. I anticipated the corresponding demands she would make of me in that first meeting; I felt completely unequipped to meet them.

This was her journey. Her determination to reconnect. To put something right, to complete unfinished business. But I didn't yet feel the same void of unfinished business. There was no conscious residual ache for me to tend. I chose to view Lizzy like a distant relative who was coming to New Zealand and wanted the chance to meet me. That much, I decided, I could handle. I would go through the polite courtesies required of the situation. I would do my best to give her what she needed, but knew very well that I might not have what she was looking for.

Chapter Three

The Baby in Her Story

'Understand the things I say
Don't turn away from me
Cause I've spent half my life out there
You wouldn't disagree

Do you see me, do you see?

Understand what I've become
It wasn't my design
And people everywhere think
Something better than I am'

'Ode To My Family,' The Cranberries

The day I met my birth mother was probably a Saturday, or perhaps a weekday during a holiday break from my teaching job at Wellington Girls' College. My memory has splintered through the years, leaving me with gaps between each detail.

Jono and my friend Jude were there to support me, but they stayed hidden in another part of the house. I couldn't say what I was wearing exactly, but it would have been nicer than on an average day. I had made an effort as you would when expecting an important guest.

Before she arrived I had made a decision – that I would do my best to be warm, to greet her with kindness. There was a moment after she knocked when I had to remind myself of that promise. I took a deep breath, composed myself, practised my forced smile that unsurprisingly wasn't coming to me naturally.

I opened the door. She was tall and slender with straight hair. We stepped toward each other. It was more than a hug, but rather a desperate grasp of her arms around me. She leaned her head into me and said, 'I just want to smell you. You are so beautiful.'

I felt like some kind of dummy. A lifeless mannequin bracing myself as she clung to me and breathed me in. I went through the motions, trying to give her what she needed, allowing her to touch me and hold me and speak to me. But at the same time, I did not peel back the gates that kept me apart from her, protected from her.

My callousness echoes even now, nearly forty years later. Why couldn't I wholeheartedly give myself to this woman, my birth mother, who wanted so desperately to hold me? But the disconnect that had started at the very moment of my birth, the rupture and separation, is not something that can be undone or forced.

Though I didn't know it at the time, the closest we could ever come to repairing that rupture would be at her hospice bedside. She would be a skeletal version of herself by the time she and I reconnected in the way she had longed for throughout her entire adult life. But at twenty-six years old, it was all I could do to practise my smile.

I invited her inside for a cup of tea at the kitchen table. We must have exchanged many words – important words – but all I remember is her excusing herself at one point to go outside for a smoke. She went out to the small garden at the back of the house and paced up and down with a cigarette in hand. It surprised me at first, seeing her give in to what appeared an anxious crutch; it must have been her way to take a break, a step back from the emotional intensity of the situation.

I had to keep repeating the reality of this meeting – that my birth mother Lizzy was there, right in front of me. I did not know how to be with her. I could feel her yearning for a deeper, heartfelt connection, for some bond of intimacy or trust to form. But she was met with a daughter doing all she could just to swallow her fear.

I felt myself rejecting her, rejecting the role I assumed she wanted me to play, rejecting her unspoken offer of connection and even love. On the surface, I was cordial, just as I would be to anyone I was meeting for the first time. As she told me stories, I filtered them out, convinced myself that they were about other people, other mothers, other babies. I couldn't allow myself to acknowledge that when she said 'my baby,' she was talking about me.

Here was the only person who could offer me truths about my life before my own memories – and all I wanted was to push her away. I feigned interest on the surface, but underneath I was silently horrified. I had empathy for her as a woman. I could see her pain and the trauma of giving me up for adoption. She was determined to overcome it, to climb out of this darkness that had enveloped her. By seeing me, telling me her story, she unburdened herself. She was relinquishing the stones in her pockets, knowing these memories must be told or they would drown her. But the freer she became, the more trapped I felt.

She expanded on the story from her letter, the story of my birth and her trauma. The words felt heavier, even more distant from me, as I heard the story again.

She was a strong young woman, and the birth was relatively straightforward. She didn't mention much about the people around her, no mother holding her hand to guide her through the pain. She had been a trainee nurse herself, so perhaps the midwife or nurses were kinder to her than they might've been to other unwed mothers at the maternity hospital. She must have had to make a decision about the adoption before she gave birth, but these were not the details we discussed. As I was born, Lizzy remembered she instinctively reached out to touch me, but they quickly bundled me away from her and said, 'You can't touch that baby. You've given it up for adoption.'

She explained that she would not leave the hospital until she had seen me. She demanded that they hold me up behind the glass window of the nursery. 'Unwrap her hands and feet,' she said, looking to ensure I had all ten toes and fingers. She looked at my eyes to see if they were both the same colour. That her daughter didn't carry her uncommon brown and green trait. It was just enough to assure herself I was 'normal,' that I would end up with a good family, and then she turned and walked away. That was the last time she saw me until she sat at my kitchen table in Newtown.

As she had told me in her letter, it was so important for her to touch me and smell me now, to finally fulfill that primal need to hold her baby. I listened, but I couldn't recognize myself as the baby in the story. That was part of the deal, my life contract, that I would be wiped clean of this pre-adoptive history – how could I possibly go back now?

In the weeks that followed, I created my own birth story in my head like a scene in a movie. A young woman on a white bed, surrounded by nurses, the midwife at the foot of the bed ready to catch the baby from her body. The mother reaching out, yearning to hold her new child. But quickly, the baby is wrapped in a linen cloth and whisked away while the mother is held down, begging for a moment to see the life she has just created. The nurse turns to her sharply, saying, 'You're not allowed to touch her.'

Despite her long telling of my birth story, there were so many pieces missing, key details that went unacknowledged. In my hesitation, my recoil of her presence in my life, my home, my existence, I doubt I had scraped for information the way I would later down the line. I still didn't even know where I was born, or who cared for me in those first few weeks of life. Lizzy had given me strips of fabric in way of a quilted blanket. I knew her experience, but none of the context.

When she left my flat, I quite literally heaved a sigh of relief. The tension in my shoulders, my arms, my neck released. But something else, something far deeper more difficult to release, had lodged itself within me.

A week later, I received a note on Massey University letterhead.

13.12.88

Dear Sue,

Thank you for sharing yourself, your husband and your home with me. At the time I felt stunned and still feel some of that, the other odd reaction was that when I came home all my posters/paintings suddenly seemed to make sense. Somehow there seemed to be a common thread after all. Strange.

All I really wanted to do was just to stare at you but I became aware of your need for information – was that true? If that was so then perhaps I can fill out a little more that was unfinished or emphasised in some points rather than others.

Then, she started to give me the 'colourful history' of a family I had never known. A great-great-grandfather who was a detective in Scotland Yard, his son a pianist refusing to follow in his father's footsteps despite the expectations of the time.

From what I gather, he 'drowned his sorrows' as they say and the solution at that time was to send the 'black sheep' out to the colonies to dry out.

This was a common narrative of that era. Just about anyone in New Zealand has heard the stories of sons who had strayed off the path getting quietly pushed off to the colonies, sent to an untamed land to match their sensibilities. I had never considered, however, that this story trope was part of my own ancestry too. My imagination concocted a creative, depressed man unsure of himself or his place in the world, shipping off to the furthest reaches of the English-speaking world where his family would never have to see him again. It was probably the worst possible solution for someone struggling. No wonder it had the opposite effect, and sent him deeper into alcoholism, as Lizzy later explained.

Not all of our family history was worrying, however. Lizzy coloured in a rough line of descendants decorated with a touch of excitement in her writing.

I believe that we can focus on any part of our heritage that we like and my favourite is our early history. My mother's sister found out that our ancestors were gypsies on the Dartmoor Moors in the 16th-17th Century which delights me somewhat. What a delicious way to live.

So, I was the descendant of alcoholic pianists, travellers, and strong-minded women. My mind had always carried me further than my feet could go, pushing my constant desire for change, for travel, for movement and adventure. I thought perhaps this restless curiosity could be an echo in my very DNA of caravaning gypsies long before my time. Lizzy went on to talk about her parents – my grandparents – and I got the sense they were part of the reason for withholding details about my own father.

I mentioned my mother to you, your grandmother, but I did not mention her strength and sheer tenacity to do more than survive and do her best for her children. She was a role model for me of those qualities, some of which I hope I have but I do have some of my father's charm too I think.

I only had a few years with him but I adored the ground he walked on. It is important to mention my father, for my relationship with my parents was an important input into my decision to decide to adopt you. It was very easy to be a demigod at 20 years of age but not possible at 46. We live and learn but sometimes at enormous cost. I withheld information on your father, for I am trying to bring him to you and that may take time hence my refusal on Saturday.

When I was pregnant with you, two men cared for me, but there was only one that I loved. The one who I thought I was pregnant to I did not tell because I knew if I did that I would have to marry him (as he wanted – without my knowledge). And I could not bear the thought of a relationship like my parents and the trouble that would bring to our child.

The other man I told I was pregnant with another man's child and he was magnificent and offered to marry me and bring you up as his own. My refusal to take up that offer was based once again on my past history. Having made those decisions I then considered my other options and these I shared with you on Saturday. The man who asked me to marry him later became my husband and in view of the former I would like your permission to give him your phone number so that he can ring you to arrange a time so that he can meet you. It is important but either of you may or may not make that choice.

Deciphering her stories was like trying to detangle a knot of string. The words appeared coded, bent around one another, used to obscure the truth as much as to reveal it. She presented a man who might be my father, who I later learned was a Greek man by the name of David Alexopolous. But then, she asked if I'd like her husband Don's phone number, implying that perhaps he was the father. The combination of adding details to avoid the primary question was a specialty of Lizzy's, as I would later come to expect. She seemed determined not to allow me to work out which one she really loved, or which one was my father.

There was something about her parents' marriage that she was anxious not to repeat. I pictured loveless years of necessary devotion, or maybe a rushed wedding due to an unplanned pregnancy.

One of her motivations for putting me up for adoption, it seemed, was to avoid a hasty or forced marriage just because of a surprise baby. Yet, as she said, the man she loved had offered to marry her even when he knew she was pregnant – and she then went on to marry him a year later anyway.

She acknowledged the confusion somewhat but didn't seem to want to make it any clearer for me.

It seems strange rereading that last paragraph for it seems like a lifetime of going over and over that decision that I made at 20. Sorting out other people's destinies and then when writing out the essentials I find that it only fills half a page.

I knew she had two children with Don, Julie and Don Junior (as she referred to him). If Don really was my father, then I would have two full siblings.

In one of our subsequent conversations, Lizzy told me she believed I was better off to not have been brought up with her, that I had escaped a difficult family life by doing so. She didn't explain what exactly she meant by that.

Lizzy had told me pieces of this story in person. She recalled once, speaking with her husband Don about her experience of adopting a baby, or perhaps telling him that she was planning to contact me. He said to her, 'If I ever find out that baby was mine, I'll shoot you.'

I have never forgotten those words and the terrifying violence they harboured and hinted at. If she knew for sure that Don was the father, she wouldn't ever make it known. It was a secret she would have kept her whole life. The first lie, perhaps she told to avoid marriage. Later, she would have to continue with it to ensure she wasn't shot for denying him the right to raise his own child. At the same time, this Don was also the man she described as 'magnificent', the one who offered to marry her and raise another man's child.

Whatever the truth, Lizzy seemed to harbour it all on her own. It must have been a heavy burden for her to bear, and in some ways, I supposed I was the only one who might be able to help her lighten it.

Sue, I'm sorry that I caused you pain and that you have experienced pain in your life and wish it was otherwise. I saw and recognised your pain but in some ways then or later when time has passed you may become or perhaps became aware that your own solutions that you came to; that the strengths you gained, were your own triumph; reflected your own mastering of two particularly difficult life events and that is something that no one can take away from you.[1]

---

[1] The life events she was referring to were my adoption and Addison's Disease diagnosis.

Chapter Four

Dead Flowers

Time smiles and whets his knife,
and something has got to come out
quickly, and be buried deep,
not spoken or thought about
or remembered even in sleep.
You must live, get on with your life.

'A Farewell,' A.R.D. Fareburn

One of the first things people ask when I tell them I'm adopted is, 'Do you know who your birth mother is? Have you met her?' It's always the mother they're interested in; the father never seems to come up.

As I've grown older, the interest in this question seems to get stronger. So often, it's the first thing people want to know about me. However, it wasn't something I was ever asked as a child. Maybe people felt it would be inappropriate in those years, when I was still actively being parented by another mother. But as an adult, away from my adopted home, the questions and the pointed curiosity have become dinner table chat.

Before I met Lizzy, it was a simple answer. I would respond, 'No I've never met her. I don't know who she is, and no, I've never tried to find her.' But once I met Lizzy, the same question became a lot harder to answer. It suddenly felt like a highly personal, invasive conversation-opener. I felt a vague sense of pressure to have a neatly-packaged story – 'Yes I have, and it was wonderful.' But I don't have a happily-ever-after story.

That fantasy is based on the idea that the underlying shame of adoption can be righted quickly, reversed. That the umbilical cord really is the only tether to this pre-adopted life. The story goes: the birth mother happily hands over her child to a better mother, a better family, and goes on to live her life relieved of the burden of an unwanted baby.

This narrative also assumes that once the baby has grown up and the mother has gone on with her life, then they can be happily reunited – two separate families become one. It all hinges on the idea that a birth mother willingly and easily releases her baby – and then willingly and easily welcomes them back twenty years later. But if we understand even a little bit about trauma, if we recognise the repercussions of wrenching a child out of a mother's hands, if we consider that in many cases the birth mothers feel they have no choice, then our perfect little daytime TV programme starts to crumble. Perhaps they exist in some cases, but I have yet to see a truly uncomplicated, happy reunion between a long lost child and a long lost mother – outside of television of course.

I avoid reading and watching those perfect accounts. They feel like watching a Disney version of reality, where all the complexity and nastiness and dark side of human nature is erased or packaged in a way that makes it easier to deal with. I feel ashamed that my narrative is not so tidy, not so happily ever after. There's a stubborn stain of shame on me that I didn't handle my first meeting with my birth mother well or do what was expected to make more of an effort.

My Mum Cicely's breezy determination to normalise the adoption of me and my sister did a good job of creating a foundation for us to grow up free of any perceived stigma. It wasn't the only force at work to help us forget. The architecture the state created to enable the removal and transfer of a baby from the illegitimate mother to the 'better' mother – the one sanctioned and protected.

The stories that we are told about adoption, however false or misleading, are so difficult to rewrite. How is it that we can be expected to forget and ignore the existence of a birth mother one day, and by the next, be waiting with open arms for a heartfelt reunion? Perhaps, in part, this was why I wrote Lizzy two months after our first meeting in such a cold, uninterested manner.

29.01.88

Dear Lizzy,

Thank you for your very generous wedding gift. We enjoy the painting as the Kapiti Coast is a favourite place of ours. Thank you too for the Christmas gifts.

Your letter was also appreciated in terms of the details you gave me about my background. The possibility of meeting your husband is not something I want to follow up and I would not want to you to give him my contact phone number. If you would like to tell me a few details about my birth father then that would be good but I do not feel I want to meet him myself.

As you are probably aware I have found the whole experience of our meeting very draining emotionally but I feel it has been positive and important that we did so. However, I don't want to continue contact in the future. I'm sorry if this is hurtful for you but while I think the reconciliation we have experienced has been healing for me, further contact would have the opposite effect. I have a strong bond with my adopted parents. They are in every way my mother and father and so it is hard for me to find room for another parent in my life.

This is a difficult letter to write (and thus the long delay in doing so) because I feel as if I am shutting the door on you. However, you have always said the initiative for our relationship would remain in my hands so I feel I can make this decision.

Thank you for finding me and having the faith to let me go as a child. I pray for God's blessing on your life always.

With love,

Sue

This is the only letter of those I wrote to Lizzy that I bothered to photocopy, and now I can see why. To this day, it fills me with shame. I had drafted something so impersonal, precisely the kind of inappropriately formal language from the State that had made me feel small and unconsidered. It was like I had followed some prescriptive formula on 'how to write a formal letter to your birth mother telling her you don't want any further contact.'

I clearly wanted to make a definitive statement and keep a formal record of that point in time – of my written intention. Was the record for me, or did I think I would need it at some future point to protect myself and prove to some third party the decision I had made?

I wonder if Lizzy ever kept my letters to her, if she had a box just like mine. But where mine tells fragments of my history, hers was a hazy peek into her future, her legacy through me. Likely, even if this box existed, it was thrown out years ago. I'll never know.

Reading back my own words over thirty years later, I hear a pompous, almost cruel voice. I wish it hadn't been mine; it is not the person I want to be. Worst of all is my self-righteous entreaty before signing off, 'I pray for God's blessing on your life always.' It was false, hollow. There I was praying for God's blessing on her while at the same time effectively cursing her. To at once deal an emotional blow and then loftily remove myself from the fallout and proclaim God's blessing on her life as she no doubt reeled from the blow. Callous, to say the least.

But as much as I wish I could say I don't recognise myself in this letter, the truth is, I do. At the time, Jonathan and I were deeply entrenched 'born again Christians' in a small breakaway charismatic church in Wellington. They had separated from the mainstream, believing they had a unique insight on the truth and the way that we should worship God.

This text reminds me of that theology – the belief in the inherent evil of the human condition and the redemptive power of Jesus. I learned to see myself as flawed and wrong, discourses that chimed well with how I already viewed myself as a young woman. I was an easy target for a theology that promised redemption from the fallible self I was all too conscious of. The stain of sin and imperfection was obvious to me as I struggled to find my place in the world as a young woman.

Every impulse tells me now to distance myself from this text, to treat it as some historic artefact from another time, another place, from a false identity. That is partly true, and yet I know I have the tendency to cut off and shut off myself from needy people and difficult emotions, to simply bring down an iron curtain and walk away feeling satisfied that I have removed myself from an emotionally painful relationship.

I have had this instinct all my life. I don't know where I learned it, but perhaps a psychologist would point out that the rupture at birth and detachment from the mother may have set this pattern deep in my psyche at a cellular level. I learned that self-protection meant cutting off or cutting out and removing some intrinsic part of myself.

Here is stark evidence of my brutality, in literal black-and-white, the evidence of my cruelty to Lizzy and of course ultimately to myself. Over the years, I have blamed my birth sister and brother for keeping me away, and I have blamed Lizzy for being secretive and protecting herself and her family from me. And yet here is evidence that, I too, at the very time I had the best opportunity to form a real connection with Lizzy, did the very opposite. I pushed her out and shut the door firmly behind her.

There is plenty of evidence to suggest that emotional and personality traits are passed down, generation to generation, just like body types or eye colour. I wonder whether some behaviours are also pre-programmed at conception, a punnet square that determines your special balance of fear and patience and selfishness and detachment. If this is true, my rejection of Lizzy could have very well been inherited from Lizzy herself. If there is one thing I know it is that my response to emotional pain leads me to disconnect and detach. The question remains – Where did I learn this?

There are no letters from Lizzy in response to mine. No doubt she retracted and tried to find a way to come to terms with this rejection. Perhaps it was the end of a fantasy of reunion she had harboured for almost thirty years.

The old flat in Newtown where Jono and I lived had a front door with a porch that we never used. We always walked past the front door and further up the concrete steps that led to another door at the back of the house where the kitchen was. About two weeks after my birthday in October and my letter to her, I went out the front door of the flat. Lying on the floor of the wooden porch was a large bunch of dead flowers from a florist wrapped in cellophane. The card read, *Dear Sue, happy birthday, with all my love Lizzy.'*

They reminded me of the dead bunches of flowers you see on freshly dug and mounded graves at the cemetery, flowers that had been on the coffin at the funeral and been carried to the graveside and left there. She hadn't told me she had sent me flowers for my birthday so I hadn't known to look out for them. It's hard to avoid the feeling that the flowers sent but not received and left to die on the front porch were symbolic of the death of the fresh hope Lizzy held for the relationship with me. But it was a hope I didn't return and so it died. There would be no flourishing of our relationship.

Now I realise that sending those flowers would have been expensive for Lizzy, a postgraduate student at Massey University. It was a gift she would have put thought and love into. She was a dedicated gardener and in the last years of her life she lived in a cottage at Highgate on the hills of Dunedin and created a beautiful garden full of roses and her beloved lilies. She was the president of the Otago Lily society for many years.

After that, there were no more gifts, and I don't know if I ever sent one to Lizzy. It was an awkward exchange. The usual reciprocal flow of gift-giving, showing love and care, had stuttered and died before it even had a chance.

Lizzy emerged for me as a lone individual in the landscape of her life, disconnected from her family and friends. Her journey was solitary by design. A newly emerged single woman, Lizzy pushed through to secure a future for herself that did not depend on the decisions of those around her. She was intent on rediscovering herself alone, and part of that was developing an isolated, contained relationship of reconciliation with me.

At the start of our reunion, I think she hoped that I would be part of her new future, but I don't think she ever expected that I would be integrated into her family of two adult children and her separated husband. There was no sense that I would be incorporated into her wider extended family either. I was her affair, her solace outside the normal routines of her life.

Someone she could visit from time to time, and then return to her life and the relationships there. I don't believe she ever wanted to merge the two dimensions of her world.

Consciously or not, I did the same thing. I told my adopted sister Wendy and a few close friends about the meeting with Lizzy and the ongoing mostly one-sided conversation through her letters, but I also kept her at a distance. I didn't want to invite her into my life, nor did I want to be drawn into what felt like an illicit one-on-one relationship. It must have disappointed and pained her to be held at arms' length like this.

Now, thirty years after that first meeting, I admire her for trying to tell me her story and her family's history. It occurs to me that I am on a very similar journey now, determined to write down what I know, to record and to honour the truth. For myself. For other adopted babies wondering whether to open their own stashed-away boxes. And of course for Max. I recognise that this work was not something I started. It began with Lizzy. And while I felt that I was left with only tangled and broken pieces, it is enough to try and weave them together to finish this half-told story.

It had been over two years since I received a dead bouquet of flowers at my doorstep when I gave birth to Max in April of 1991. Max's birth was a long labour complicated by my chronic autoimmune disorder, Addison's disease. Diagnosed in my twenties, I knew that Addison's disease made me particularly susceptible to stressors and illness. I had always wondered if it was a hereditary disorder, but Lizzy had confirmed to me early in our letters that there was no trace of it in her family line.

I went into labour after drinking half a bottle of castor oil to get things started, as I was past my due date and there was talk of an induction if I didn't go into labour in the next twenty-four hours. The castor oil did the trick and Jono and I headed to Wellington Hospital with our friend and midwife, Mary. Things started well but the labour slowed down. They hooked me up to a Syntocinon drip to artificially stimulate labour. Max was born in the early morning with me determined to avoid a Caesarean section as he was in the posterior position which made birthing difficult. I remember making a herculean effort to push him out, possible only with a good-sized episiotomy cut, without anaesthetic, and a lot of stitches to repair the damage.

As Max emerged, he was swiftly wrapped and delivered into my arms. At that moment, I thought of Lizzy. I finally understood the weight of this most profound and powerful birthing process, and the overwhelming emotion and connection I felt for Max, this new being of my being. She must have felt all of these feelings too, but without the chance to realise them. While I was able to hold Max and breastfeed him immediately after birth, Lizzy saw nothing but an anonymous bundle taken away from her bedside. I suddenly understood the impact of that separation on her.

Despite my earlier letter to Lizzy saying I wanted no further contact, I knew then that the right thing to do was to reach out to her and share the news of Max's birth. A few months later, I received a letter in return.

19.08.91

Dear Sue & Jonathan & Max,

My congratulations to you all. This is a very quick delighted response – probably because I have just received your card & photo. I see you had posted it in April- the current tenants in my old house must have finally sent it on. I had sent you a postcard with my change of address but not till about May I think.

I have moved to Taupo & now work for the Justice Dept in the prisons & have been here since early March. I would like to send something to celebrate Max's arrival. How would that be for you?

In the meantime – I am delighted – I hope Sue that all went well, both pregnancy and labour. Well done, my love to you all.

Lizzy Mackenzie

Her relief of reconnection is palpable. Despite my harsh, determined words and my 'God Bless You,' the door had not yet completely sealed shut. She wanted to take it further, to actively try to stitch time back together. But it wasn't what felt important to me at the time. She offered to send a gift to Max, but I didn't reply. More than just getting caught in the overwhelming first few weeks of being a parent, I simply didn't feel the need for anything more.

When Max was born, my mum Cicely was right there next to me. She and Dad were so excited about the birth, so excited to become grandparents. They had never experienced those first few days in the hospital before, and it was such a visceral experience for all of us to share in it together. Max had his grandparents. I had a mother supporting me. There just wasn't any space left for Lizzy to fill.

Looking back at it now, I realise that I hadn't considered truly what Max's birth meant to Lizzy. That she was also now a grandmother. That she might be curious and even have love for her grandson. I was playing by the rules she set out back when I first held that cut-out photo of her – *this is just me and you.* I wouldn't involve myself in her family, and she wouldn't involve herself in mine. It was important at the time to tell her about the birth itself, but it had hardly crossed my mind that she would see herself as a grandmother to Max.

When I didn't reply, our correspondence dissolved. It would be another seven years before I received another letter – enough time for both of our lives and our perspectives to shift.

CHAPTER FIVE

All We Shared Was an Umbilical Cord. It Was Cut.

You do not have to be good.
You do not have to walk on your knees
for a hundred miles through the desert repenting.
You only have to let the soft animal of your body
love what it loves.
Tell me about despair, yours, and I will tell you mine.

'Wild Geese,' Mary Oliver

My life in the late-90s was full of major transitions. Two years after Max was born, Jono and I had a fraught and painful separation. I began to establish a new path as a single mum, and decided to continue studying for my masters and then my doctorate at Victoria University.

With no car and only a small income from PhD scholarships and a bit of tutoring, guest lecturing and research work, living in Wellington became increasingly difficult. Max and I were both unhappy in our small, damp basement rental flat and the relationship with Jono was difficult and adversarial. He was not as supportive or available as I needed him to be. Just after Max's fifth birthday, with Jono's agreement, I made the decision for us to move to Taupō to live with Mum and Dad.

In hindsight, it was a good decision, but it meant another move for Max from our first family home in Karori, to a basement flat in Hataitai, and then to Taupō. Max loved living with Granny and Grandad, who gave us a loving, stable home after a few difficult years.

Within a year of living in Taupō, I managed to buy a small cottage across the road from Mum and Dad with my share of the equity from the first home that Jono and I had owned in Karori. Our days became routine. I would cycle Max to school, him sitting on the carrier of my bike. When I got home, I would settle into the living room with the open fire in winter to write my PhD, then bike back to pick him up after school. In the summer we'd zoom past the cottage down the two blocks to the lake. There were three letters from Lizzy during this time, and we began speaking on the phone somewhat regularly.

We kept each other updated about our travels.

> *Kayaking in the Sounds would be beautiful, we once had a boating holiday there and I fell in love with the area.*

She asked after my studies, always interested in hearing about the world I was uncovering in academia. Lizzy had gone back to school, and our studies were something we had in common. She even sent me journal articles, recommended books, and asked after specific papers.

> *I was impressed with your thesis title. I was only able to squeeze in one feminist paper during my BA degree but I really enjoyed it. Try to keep up with some of the feminist reading from the library but somehow I always seem to stagger out with more gardening books.*

It became a more familial exchange. We had gotten over some of the stuffy, formal tone and now, she was just checking in like a friend or an Auntie.

> *Well, just a note to keep in touch, & to wish you well in your final run down to your PhD completion. Don't forget to look at the sky (even if it is buried behind the computer screen of the window) & dream.*

She kept me updated about her life, too. The time spent in her garden, or working on the house.

> *Still into house renovations or should I say massive earth moved from back to front and back again! The driveway is now in & I thought I had been cunning with earthworks but the poor soil is in transit once again. Once the verandah is on (in about a month) then that should be it & the garden I've developed will be it and I will <u>have</u> to reduce that 500 lilies & 100 roses into a tiny section that definitely will <u>not</u> go. Ho hum.*

I could picture her in the garden of her cottage, keeping track of her precious flowers as the renovations progressed inside. There she was, meticulously counting each budding rose bush, cataloguing this careful beauty she had nurtured. By this point, Lizzy had been separated from her husband Don for many years, but when his health declined, she put her PhD at Otago University on hold to look after him. I can't remember what I was told about his health, but I found it strange that she had returned to Don after being separated for so long. It was clear she felt some kind of responsibility to give up her academic pursuits to care for him in his hour of need. I wondered if there was an element of repayment; he had stuck by her when she disappeared from the family while she was mentally unwell, and perhaps this was the time she could say thank you. I started to get regular updates about Don and his slow but steady decline.

> *Don's health is stable but still not OK enough for me to go back to uni so I will have a look at it again at the beginning of next year.*

At the other end of the country, I was in my little cottage in Taupō, with a vegetable garden and flower gardens of roses and old-fashioned pink dahlias. As autumn went on, we started chatting on the phone. She asked after my garden; I asked about my birth father. The letters became longer, as she began to unravel the family history.

I have done a lot of thinking since your call... The initial glitch I think is that you & I don't have a common shared history. Putting aside the emotional factors – all we shared was an umbilical cord. It was cut. Your history was gathered and developed within your family..

So it was with me – I am not unencumbered. I too am a product of my family history. I can make strong statements like 'I shall be the gatekeeper' etc. because of the conditioning process by two powerful matriarchs – my mother and my grandmother.

I was struck by these words, 'All we shared was an umbilical cord. It was cut.' Despite her desperation to hold me, to smell me, to reconnect and repair, she holds onto the fiction of the state – that once a baby is born the connection between the mother and child is cleanly, neatly severed. Yet Lizzy's desire to connect with me as an adult told another story. Despite her efforts to hide her pregnancy and my birth and go on to create a life for herself with another family of her own, the connection lingered until she finally wrote to me when she left her marriage.

She said her actions were a result of her matriarchal conditioning, a 'product of family history'. In the same letter, she gave a short history of the two 'powerful matriarchs' in her life and the inheritance of trauma and lack of attachment that she was conditioned and shaped by.

Her London-born grandmother married an alcoholic, a 'black sheep', the male heir of the family, who was sent to the colonies to dry out. The disconnection and isolation had the opposite effect. Here was the beginning of a pattern: the response to anyone who brought shame on the family was to send them away, distance them from the rest of the family, and then cover it up with lies.

The impact on Lizzy's grandmother was the experience of entrapment and isolation. Lizzy's mother, 'repeated the same scenario.' I assumed Lizzy meant that her mother also married an alcoholic and had to struggle to survive, and I wondered if Don, Lizzy's husband, could have been the same. Grandmother, mother and daughter, all following the same path. A marriage that shouldn't have happened. The shame of their husbands. Ongoing, persistent depression to follow.

The impact of the Second World War on Lizzy's mother, my grandmother, was two-fold. On the day Lizzy was born, Christmas Day, her mother received the news that her two beloved younger brothers had been killed in the war, a shock that surely would have impacted her ability to bond with her new daughter.

Lizzy's father was also away at war for four years, leaving her mother to raise her two children alone. He returned needing hospital and home care and left the family 'several years later' when Lizzy would still have been quite young. She had raised two children on her own, abandoned by her husband, without her brothers.

The damage in the family line ran like a seam in a landscape showing the ruptures and layers of generations past. I was born in shame, taken away within minutes of my first breath. Lizzy and I both were denied that chance to bond in those previous early days of motherhood and life. But Lizzy too was born surrounded by chaos, trauma, fear. Her first day would have been marked by news of the death of her uncles and her first years would have been stigmatised by a father who left. Despite Lizzy's assertion that we didn't 'have a common shared history' I wondered what impact these traumas had on me as the eldest daughter in her family line even though I was transplanted into another family?

So much of Lizzy's story felt familiar. It was a history of failed attachment and abandonment, echoing my own life. It was as if I had been swimming against currents I could not see, not understanding that it had taken me greater energy than most to form loving attachments. I was frightened by the power of this history and the way it might have shaped my life.

Soon after came a sense of wonder. How did I manage to swim against these currents all these years? I was always a strong swimmer. I still swim a couple of kilometres at a time in the sea around Waiheke Island, even in winter. But these dark waters, the history and the rejection, were entirely different. I wondered if it would have been better not to know any of these details, just as the state determined when it set up closed adoption policies. After all, the rules were intended to protect us, the unwanted babies, from our past. To offer a clean history with a new adopted family, untainted by the sins of the foremothers and fathers. Lizzy had thought about these things too. In one of her letters, she wrote:

> *Society has rules, and the original rules under which you were adopted were clear. That is, you were protected from me for you and your family's best interests. With hindsight, society has dealt with some of the draconian aspects & has made some amendments. The adult adopted child can now access information they require to gain genetic or some sense of hereditary/lineage information etc.*
>
> *This has been done with good intent for the best interests of the child <u>not</u> the birth mother. I pushed the amendment to its limits to get my own needs met – and one of my prime motives would have been to assuage guilt I'm sure. The outcome of that meeting in fact made me realise it may not have been in your best interests.*

It clearly weighed on her. The need to repair, the impossibility of doing so without causing further damage. The guilt. No doubt, Lizzy had considered what her actions meant to the people around her. Perhaps that was why her stories always left gaps, and her answers never truly offered a conclusion. The state had taught her that protection meant concealing the truth. She felt she had pushed the law to its limits for her own gain by reaching out to me and putting forth information I hadn't asked for. Her attempt to repair our relationship was at direct odds with the clean break that was expected from birth mothers. She had seen how difficult this reconnection was for me, and she was in a battle between filling her own needs and still trying to protect me. The battle was everywhere, playing out in her explanations, her stories, her letters.

> *Anyway my mother did a damn fine job of bringing me up in spite of all the stigmas operating in society at that time. And to find out that I had strayed from the straight & narrow was a shock for her.*
>
> *So this is where you come in. For better or worse with the facts I had at that time and 98 percent sure that David was the father, I made a decision which I thought was in everyone's best interests.*
>
> *I told Don at that time it was not his child. His offer to marry*

me & raise the child as his own was rejected. Later I did marry
Don & for the next 20 years or so you were my business not his, nor
my children's. When I met you it still remained my business as Don
and I were pending divorce. Fate has intervened & now he & I are
together while I care for him. My current assumption is 98 percent
in his favour – but the usual curse for males – can one be sure? The
only certainty is what comes from a woman's womb. That we can be
sure of. So that is one of the premises which inhibits me.

This letter confirms her earlier account of the predicament she found
herself in when she was pregnant with me. At the time of my conception
and for many years afterwards she says she believed that David was my
father. In this letter she says that she now believes the truth is '98 percent'
in Don's favour. To this day, I'm not sure why she came to that conclusion.
I wonder if she had started to see traits in me that reflected her husband.
Yet, she maintains that I was her business – not his. Lizzy kept her growing
relationship with me secret from Don, her separated husband, believing
that he was not my father.

The other factor is the critical one, for me anyway. What we have
are a cluster of adults, all complex with their own needs & wants, all
within relationships and getting on with their own business. And I
am not only including my own family but yours too. Your sister may
think she has exclusive rights – I don't know and I certainly cannot
imagine how your parents would feel or do feel.

But I do know how I feel. I cannot make any more decisions that
will affect other people. And the fact of the matter is that I no longer
have that right, legally or morally.

So, where that leaves you Sue I don't know. But the little I do
know of you says you are highly intelligent and very articulate, and
you will probably let me know.

Her reluctance to act on her growing belief about my birth father's identity
was based on her desire to protect everyone. She was gatekeeping, trying
to protect her children and their father from the truth that I could actually

be Don's daughter. She suggested my adopted sister Wendy might feel she has 'exclusive rights' to me. I assume she meant that Wendy would not want to know I have another sister, that this would somehow dislodge our relationship and my relationship with my adopted parents.

Unbeknown to Lizzie, Wendy was going on her own journey of discovery of her birth family and history. Unlike me, she was the one who searched for and found her birth mother and birth father. Unlike me, her story was one of welcome and ongoing connection with her birth parents and her other siblings. What we had in common was a sense of privacy, an unspoken agreement that these were discoveries we had to make alone and shared only a little with Mum and Dad and a little more with each other. Over time and since Mum and Dad have died, we have spoken more about our birth histories and I have met Wendy's birth mother and sisters. Wendy has always been a safe place for me, the one who understands and believes in my right to know about my birth parents.

What struck me was Lizzy's attention to this underlying idea of ownership, as if I was property transferred from her to another family and could not hold both histories or belong to two families at the same time. As if they were mutually exclusive options – being a member of my adopted family precluded rights to also belong to my birth family.

She concluded that she could no longer hold these tensions, no longer stand as the moral arbiter holding everyone's secrets in her hands. Yet, she didn't go on to tell me everything. She recognised this gate where she stood guard, and abandoned her post. The rest was up to me.

It took me months. My desire to know battled with my fear of further rejection. I didn't know if I could handle discovering another gate in this journey only to find I was barred entry.

Eventually, I took the contact information Lizzy had handed over, and started with the '98% sure' potential father. If that proved unsuccessful, I told myself, I would call Don. I chose my words carefully. Clear, steady, but holding my breath at every syllable.

Dear David.

I am writing to introduce myself to you and to ask of you a very great favour. Please allow me to explain.

I told him a bit about me, and Lizzy, and included a photo, wondering if it would spark some memory for him. Then, I tried as simply as I could to tell him why I was writing.

In early 1962 Lizzy was living in Wellington and was involved with two men one of whom she tells me was you. She became pregnant and went to Auckland to give birth – apparently without your knowledge. Lizzy tells me that she believes there is a '98% chance' that you are my father.

I am writing to ask for your help to determine who my father is. The other man who Lizzy was involved with at the time is terminally ill and because of his frail condition and because Lizzy believes it is most likely that you are my father I am reluctant to approach him at this time. I know nothing of your circumstances but I imagine that receiving this letter is quite a shock. Lizzy remembers you as a good man – may I prevail upon your goodness to ask you to meet with me to help me with my search for my birth father?

Two weeks later, after an anxious wait, I received a reply in the mail. On the front of the envelope, alongside my name and address was written, 'PERSONAL AND CONFIDENTIAL.'

Dear Susan,

During the past week or so, since receiving your letter, I have been trying to come to grips with your news, decide how I feel about this, and the possible repercussions.

After much soul searching I decided I would rather not know either way. I don't say this is in a callous or unfeeling way because from your letter I assume you to be a nice person. I don't want to hurt your feelings but neither do I want to do anything that may jeopardise the wellbeing of my family. I really believe that taking it further whatever the outcome will create problems rather than solve them.

He was kind, but the answer was hurtful. He gave his reasons for this decision to not engage, explaining that his family had been through a horrible tragedy not long before and was still grieving. Then he ends the letter:

I cannot let my family go through another major emotional destruction, I know I cannot face another one. I would rather the past remained to the past. I do hope you understand.

No one had ever told me so directly, but it was a tune that felt familiar: my existence was something painful, something better left forgotten. I am sure he struggled to write this letter, to make the decision about whether to open this door into his family. I replied, again careful to not be accusatory or let on too much emotion. Before I signed off, I told him he was welcome to contact me again if he changed his mind.

I wouldn't know for another twenty years whether David really was my father or not. In the meantime, I just had Lizzy. And she was more interested than ever to show me that we could build some kind of relationship, that we did have common ground. She signed off one of her letters assuring me that there was another inheritance I received from her; along with the trauma, a 'fierce independence and ability to make decisions.' Then, a list of all the good things I would have inherited from her gene pool. All the things, I suppose, I would have gotten before that umbilical cord was cut.

Now one final footnote: You know the negative stuff re: autoimmune system rogue genes. Let me tell you the consistent/persistent positive characteristics that abound in our family..

Longevity (would you believe!)
Physical strength & fitness

Articulate ++
Tenacious +++!
Hard workers
Selective perfectionists
Very curious
Lateral thinkers
Courageous
Loyal ++
Caring & compassionate
Vivacious
Outrageous sense of humour!

Chapter Six

A Storm in a Teacup

'Nothing that is in equilibrium can be alive.'

Storm in a Teacup: The Physics of Everyday Life, Helen Czerski

All the time spent writing my PhD thesis next to my cosy cottage fireplace had paid off. After working on an educational research project that made quite a splash overseas, I was lucky to have my pick of research associate roles at two Ivy League universities in the US. The two year contract at the University of Pennsylvania paid more than the one at Harvard, a key decision factor as a single mum at the time. So, we packed up, and began a new chapter in Philadelphia.

Life was not easy for Max and I in that first year. I hadn't quite finished revisions on my thesis, so between a full time job, guest lecturing in the Graduate School of Education, and finalising my own research, there wasn't much extra time to spend with my eight-year-old who was just learning to figure things out in a new country. I was often travelling to other cities to conduct my research, so I left Max with a caregiver, a graduate student who would stay with him in our apartment for two or three day stretches at a time.

I could see Max was stressed; I was too. It felt terrible leaving him like that, and I became so anxious that I would have nightmares about him being kidnapped or getting lost in the subway. Though I was on the cusp of something incredibly important with my research, I knew the set-up wasn't sustainable for Max.

At the end of the year, I decided it was best for him to go back to New Zealand and live with his father until my contract was finished and I could return home. I flew with him to Los Angeles, so that I could watch him board the flight for Auckland. Over the next year, I travelled back to New Zealand a few times during his school holidays. But the distance was difficult for everyone.

Max and I had a standing daily phone call the entire time we were apart – which meant unlimited international minutes set up on my plan. With so much of my life now tethered with phone calls, it was only natural that Lizzy and I started speaking more regularly. Philadelphia gave me the safe distance that I needed. We spoke about our relationships with men, New Zealand neo-liberal politics, psychology and literature. She slid into the role of a wise aunt; we were two feminist academics taking on questions of existence.

Lizzy was incredibly proud of my academic career, how my move to Philadelphia 'took her breath away' and how wonderful it was that I had landed a 'crème de la crème' position. She told me that she only studied for a PhD for a short time, 'But I do remember the isolation and trying to ferret out people who knew grammar! Or could explain some weird scientific formulas.'

Looking back, I admire myself too over this time. I'm astounded to have managed it all – the workload, the parenting responsibilities from 14,000 kilometres away, connecting with Lizzy. The freshness of a new city also helped me open my eyes. I got to explore in a way I hadn't been able to in the cloistered Christian days of my early-twenties.

There were eight letters sent over this period of time to Philly. Re-reading them now, I see two independent women embracing the curiosity of life. Across the Pacific Ocean, Lizzy was discovering her 'green fingers,' pouring her heart into the flowers that dotted her piece of Highgate, up the hill from Dunedin.

We are into autumn harvesting of the vege patch and I have sunflower heads drying all over the place (they feed the birds in the winter), pumpkins stalked, potatoes drying out, ropes of garlic and onions so the kitchen has a French-Provençal flavour!

The lilies she grew from seed were 'magnificent'. Her dedication grew as quickly as her flowers, and she was soon appointed editor of the Otago Lilly Society Bulletin. In one of her letters she sent me, her first issue as editor, she says, 'The three hundred spring bulbs of daffodils and tulips were a vibrant floriferous display.'

The roses are fleshing out so I imagine chaos once everything else is up and then I'll be grizzling that all needs culling. Oh the joys of gardening.

To 'keep herself sane' she started a garden stall at the front gate selling lilies and other flowers with the aim of buying garden furniture so that the garden would pay for itself. She was in her late fifties then, had spent much of her adult life in study, and with Don undergoing radiotherapy treatment, I assumed finances were tight.

By the end of 1999, Julie, her daughter, had bought her parents a 'flash' new computer. Lizzy told me she was looking forward to 'surfing the net with gay abandon.' Don drew up a Christmas letter on the computer, which she sent along my way. She was also proud to report that the garden stall had returned a thousand dollars, enough to pay for the new garden furniture.

More and more, I started to hear about Don on our calls and through our letters. Despite early success with the treatment, the end of the millennium was spent in the oncology ward at Dunedin hospital while they awaited a decision 'as to a chop or chemo.' Lizzy had opened a window for me to peer in and see Don, Julie, and Don Jr. But as it turned out, they hadn't been told much at all about me. Despite our developing relationship, Lizzy was still a one-way mirror, my existence a hazy figure in the background to her 'actual' children.

Now I would love to welcome you through the front door, banners flying, yellow ribbons round the old oak tree, brass bands, flowers and champagne as the family hug and draw you into our home. But that is the stuff of fairy tales. As we all know only visitors and strangers enter by the front door, family come in through the back.

You are well in the back door. However this door usually opens into the scullery and that's probably where we are and one chore that needs to be done is to go through the dirty linen. Perhaps then you will understand my reluctance and concern for Julie and Don Jnr.

When it came to her children, the doors were closed. But her own history – that was an open book, it seemed.

I grew up with my Mum who was depressed most of the time. I have found that most people who are depressed have remarkable survival skills but poor living skills. I of course took those on board. As the years went by and the stresses stacked both those skills/non-skills were tested to the full with the predicted outcome. I can't even remember what the final stress was that tipped me over, but one day I was a fully functioning wife and mother and the next day I was in a psychiatric unit. I was an accident waiting to happen and when it did, unfortunately it was my family who got lumbered. For 18 months I was very unwell and spent about nine months in psychiatric units. I was drugged up to the gills and unable to help my family through this time. They were given no explanations or help so they got on as best they could – and they did just fine.

However, I got lucky when someone had the bright idea of sending me south, fortunately to a private psych unit. They had not only moved on from the medical model, but were able to make a correct diagnosis, educated me and gave me insight into what was going on, taught me some good living skills and I came back home well and have never looked back since. Unfortunately the marriage relationship deteriorated over time with the result that I left the family a couple of years later. There were therefore two episodes that both children were exposed to where their world as they knew it fell apart. They are both remarkable human beings but perhaps you can now understand my ambivalence about exposing them to a situation that may have unpredictable outcomes.

I suppose I was the unpredictable outcome. The mere existence of me was something that caused pain.

> *But all is not lost. During my discussions about you with Don, I asked again if he would meet you. His reply was that he was willing to meet you. Now both J and D not only adore their father but also think he is the measure of all that is logical, rational and sensible. If he meets you and all is well that could lead to the next step of approaching them again. With that kind of climate there may be a better chance of a positive outcome and especially, less chance of you getting hurt too Sue. Your welfare is one of my prime concerns and I hope your exposure to additional information about myself has caused you no further distress. However in my opinion it is our limitations rather than our strengths, which make us unique individuals and develop our humaneness.*
>
> *Well I think that is enough pontificating, and drama. Now, I happen to like sculleries and one usually finds some interesting things in them, apart from dirty linen! Tools and bits and bobs are there also. With the right tools (which I think we both have) and the necessary nuts and bolts I think we can open the rest of the doors – but once you have seen my kitchen you may regret that!*

She concluded the letter:

> *Sue, I think it is time I went outside and considered the lilies and how they grow. I wish you a splendid and exciting new millennium and may your challenges be energising as well as much easier than you thought.*

I thought of Julie and Don Jr, and what it would have been like for them to have a mother disappear due to mental illness. I imagined Don taking over all the parenting duties, the strength it would have taken for the entire family to be compassionate and supportive and move past this period of time. I had experienced mental illness myself not long after my marriage, but thankfully had the expertise of a feminist psychiatrist, and coping skills that I learned from my Mum and Dad growing up. Perhaps the illness was inherited, but I had always assumed my resilience was learned.

This time would have brought Don very close to his children. It was no wonder that he was greatly loved and admired. This was the man who might be my father, I reminded myself. He began to come into focus in my mind, but I wasn't yet ready to meet him. 'I'll shoot you if I find out that baby is mine' echoed in my head. And the sting from David's rejection was still fresh.

I recognised that Lizzy was trying to get out of the way between me and whoever my father was. In the spirit of opening up our lives just a little further, I offered the chance for her to meet Max.

Lizzy's response wasn't what I expected:

> *Now, I have thought long and hard about Max and me – or our relationship per se. Grandchildren are precious and I think his grandparents and him need an uncomplicated relationship. Due to adoptive issues I imagine there have been difficult times with their respective daughters with birth parents involved, one way or the other. Secondly, I don't think I can cope with seeing him then having no further or minimal contact. I find the older I get the less able I am to deal with emotional loss/grief etc and would find it a kind of subtle torture etc. That notwithstanding, when Max is an adult, and should he make a decision under his own volition that he does wish to meet me, for whatever reason, I am more than happy to see him.*

I wish I could go back and charge through the door, just make it happen. But I felt paralysed, unable to act, scared that a stronger rejection would hurt too much. She saw the potential pain it would bring Max, and the complicated feelings it would likely bring her too. We had come so far, so many words exchanged and secrets unearthed, but our connection was still so fragile. In the same letter, she revealed to me that Don wasn't the only one facing a health decline.

21.05.00

My health is all turning out to be a storm in a teacup.

Query reflux oesophagitis was the result of the gastroscopy, which about half of the population have at one time or another so on antacids and they will take out my gallbladder when it plays up again so all is well. All other hypotheses have been debunked at this time (apart from an old back injury) so onward and upward. Sue, don't worry too much about family genetics etc. Don Jnr is as fit as a buck rat evidenced by his completion of 3 ironmans which he did in great times and Julie uses the world as her playground and anything that is exciting, difficult and dangerous, her and her partner charge off to it – and you need to be damn fit and well to do some of the hair raising things she gets up to.

Just a few months later, in August of 2000, I got the message that Don senior had died. I had waited too long. It had all happened too fast. I had meant to contact Don eventually, once the wound from David had healed over, but I hesitated too long. I realised then – and I realise even more now – just how many lost opportunities for connection there had been. I had taken up so few of those moments, and now it was too late.

Despite her assertion that longevity runs in the family, the man who could be my father died of cancer in his mid-sixties. Of course, we didn't know at the time, but within a few short years, Lizzy would also be diagnosed with cancer.

CHAPTER SEVEN

A Gift or a Destiny

Ah, love, let us be true
To one another! For the world, which seems
To lie before us like a land of dreams,
So various, so beautiful, so new,
Hath really neither joy, nor love, nor light,
Nor certitude, nor peace, nor help for pain;
And we are here as on a darkling plain
Swept with confused alarms of struggle and flight,
Where ignorant armies clash by night

'Dover Beach', Matthew Arnold

After my contract in Philadelphia finished, Max and I were back living in Wellington. Familiar city, completely new life. This time I rented an apartment at Oriental Bay, fulfilling a promise to myself that when I returned to New Zealand I would live by the sea. Max was twelve, commuting to school in Karori on the bus, and visiting his dad nearby. I had funds from selling our Taupō cottage, and a consultant job to help support us through a new mortgage when we were eventually able to buy our own home around the corner in Mount Victoria. We were rebuilding, and it felt like the right direction.

Things with Lizzy, however, didn't fit neatly into that new direction. Without the safe distance cast by the Pacific Ocean, I felt the uncomfortable tug again into a still-uncertain relationship. As I had done the last time I was living in Wellington, I pulled away, and there were a couple years of sparse communication. It wasn't until 2003 that we resumed writing to one another.

04.01.03

Dear Sue

I am twice blessed. The photo you sent of you and your sister and respective sons was lovely. Thank you. And now to actually see your parents! I knew they could only be the best, when I first saw you, your excellent upbringing was apparent. My one thought when I read the article and saw the photo was that I was one lucky woman, way back all those years ago.

I hope the house hunting is going well and in the not too distant future you will have your own home to savour and enjoy...

Sue, thank you.

My love, Lizzy

I remember sending Lizzy a photo of Mum and Dad taken on their fiftieth wedding anniversary by the local Taupō paper who published a story about them. I still have a copy of that framed photo on my dressing table. They are laughing and leaning against each other, their love and connection still apparent in their late seventies. Lizzy was right – they were the best. She was lucky that I had been adopted by Cicely and Peter. And so was I.

In the time we had been off speaking terms, Lizzy's health had declined significantly. She had been in hospital after severe haemorrhoids when they found an extremely rare instance of cancer:

Things were not good and about mid April, they put me in hospital and discovered a small cell cancer of the anal floor. It is extremely rare at that site, which is why they never thought of it. They immediately put me on chemotherapy and I am now in the process of having radiotherapy with chemo starting up once they finish the former.

In her letter, she put on a brave face. I could see her determination to be cheery about the service at the hospital, the seventy to eighty percent success rate of her chemotherapy treatment, and of course she was anxious to reassure me that this particular cancer is not hereditary.

Despite her positive thinking, the cancer progressed quickly. I believe it took her by surprise. The next letter I received from her, less than a year later, was postmarked from Dunedin Hospice.

Dearest Sue,

Finally, finally getting to see the wood for the trees or is it the other way around? I shall repeat what I said on the phone, my abject apologies for not acknowledging your lovely flowers sooner. They were a lovely bunch of spring flowers with gerberas and many a nurse poked their nose in to trace the ... fragrance. Thanks to both you and Max. Being sick has been hectic, been at 8c (oncology ward hospital) and now at the hospice. The pain is proving a sod to get on top of it but got the night time sorted so halfway there. Now I will decrease some and up some others to find which are the critical drugs and then put them in pill form and <u>then</u> home! Will email you as soon as home. Once again thank you.

My love to you and Max, Lizzy. Xx

I wish I could remember the things I had told her during this time, what future plans I had divulged that were so meaningful to her. I cannot even remember sending those flowers. It meant a lot that she continued to sign off cards to Max. Despite never choosing to meet him, he was certainly on her mind.

It became clear over these next few weeks that Lizzy wasn't going to make it home. What happened next I can't say with complete certainty. I don't remember how it all happened, or even how many times I visited her. This period of time is like looking back into early childhood memories, flashes and moments interspersed with long stretches of hazy speculation.

I look back into the box for clues, and find an entry in my journal:

Thursday 2 September 2004: I flew to Dunedin for the day.

I have no memory of this. Trauma is a powerful thing. It can erase moments in history, a biological protection response. The pieces of writing drafted during this time are my tethers to the truth, enabling me to tape together the story. It started with Mum writing a letter to Lizzy saying thank you. I took this letter down with me to deliver it in person. A few days later, Lizzy sent a response.

4.09.04

Dear Cicely and Peter,

What a lovely thought & card. You may think Sue as a gift but I regard it as destiny, it was meant to happen. And Sue had number one parents and the efforts show in her behaviour and her vocabulary. I could never have given to Sue which you were both able to provide. She is an independent, assertive and ambitious woman but her natural attributes soften those credentials. (Please excuse my writing but the drugs I am on are hard on the poor old brain)

I wish both you and your family my best wishes for now and the future.

Regards, Lizzy

I love that Mum wrote to Lizzy, knowing she was dying, wanting to thank her for her gift. Before it was too late, Mum took the time to acknowledge everything Lizzy had done for her family. Thank you Mum.

There are other pieces of paper from this time. There's a second letter to Mum and Dad saying the same words of thanks, perhaps a result of Lizzy forgetting she had sent the first – a symptom of the intensive medication she was on. I had written an email to my friends and family, updating them on the experience.

> *Just a note to say thank you for your support over this time as I reconnect with my birth mother, Lizzy, and spend time with her as she prepares to die. I spent a couple of hours with her at the hospice in Dunedin yesterday. Our time was strong and special – she wanted to talk and tell me about her life and her history and her family, and she asked about mine. I know she was in a lot of pain but she is strong willed and stayed awake for the 2 hours I was with her – a mammoth effort considering the high doses of pain relief she is on.*
>
> *She said the oncologist asked her, 'How do you feel about dying?' And she said, 'Great doc, I'm ready to go. I've had a chaotic full life and I'm ready to go.' To me she said there is only one thing she has to do – to forgive herself: for adopting me and for other things she didn't talk about. Yet she says she has no regrets. She assures me she will do this work of forgiveness before she passes over.*

In the same email, I also acknowledged that I had a phone call with my half-sister, Julie. There was a touch of joy, of hope in the connections I was forming despite the pain of seeing Lizzy deteriorate. The experience had brought my walls down; I had hoped it would for Julie too.

Nearly a month later, I received a card with a white camellia by Georgia O'Keeffe on the cover. Her writing was messy compared to her usual style.

29.09.04

Dear Susanne

It was great to see you. You continue to present a real vibrancy, a rare quality. Thank you very much for the Annie Dillard book. I have not yet read it (see below as to why) but it will be the first on my list when the brain functions again properly. I had a period of a few days when I went quite 'ga ga' everyone... Hence all the muddling stupid Q & As you must have got. My apologies. I am just going to write a short note to your mother in response to your card. I hope that is OK. Thank you for telling me your plans for the future, may each and every one come true.

Sue my love to you & Max

Thank you for taking the time and trouble.

Go well, Lizzy

She called me 'Susanne,' not Susan. It was as if her memory was breaking down right in front of me under the ravages of cancer. Pieces of her consciousness decomposing, moments of her remembered life slowly losing their way.

It would have taken so much determination through the immeasurable pain and the strong drugs to keep her mental acuity, to muster the courage to pick up a pen. But she did. That's the kind of woman Lizzy was.

CHAPTER EIGHT

The Current of Love

Write as if you were dying...What could you say to a dying person that would not enrage by its triviality?

The Writing Life, Annie Dillard

I've heard it said that the body remembers, that memories are held in our cells and our unconscious. They can be triggered by the quality of light in a season, biological clues like roses in bloom, the building pressure of hot summer days. This is the time of year when I saw Lizzy at her deathbed in Dunedin for the last time. Where I had lost my memory of my first trip, this one remains in my consciousness. It is a stone I have been searching for for a long time. When I turned it over, I realised I was the one who had thrown it so far away. The start of the end was an email from Julie.

12.12.04

Harsh as it sounds it may be that we are nearing the end and I thought I should give you some warning.

I flew down, once again, to Dunedin. It was December, and the city was quiet with the students already home for the year. The hospice building was just outside the city centre, right next to the world's steepest street. If you climbed to the top of it, you could look down on the hospice where inside, in every bed, people were making their final climb.

I noticed flowers everywhere – blooming alongside the road, roses by the automatic doors to the hospice building, bouquets at the reception counter. A middle-aged woman smiled at me from behind the desk, in that warm, but clinical space that said 'Don't be afraid. You can come in here and be amongst the dying, it's all right.'

I walked towards Lizzy's room with a sense of fear about what I would find. Her room was large and light, a kind of green glow all around her. One bed with a chair on each side and a small round table. A sliding door that opened to a paved courtyard with an outdoor table and chairs and a grassy bank leading down to a stream. To the right, the stream continued on and then disappeared under the road. Ducks, common brown mallards, made their way up from the stream across the grassy bank to the courtyard, quacking and waddling and shitting.

I sat at Lizzy's bedside on a visitor chair. The bed was elevated and she was propped up with pillows. They had stopped trying to cure her; the drugs were given only to keep her comfortable. She had stopped eating and drinking, and there were tubes coming out of her body. One dripped slowly into a bag half-filled with dark urine.

It smelled of death, her body already breaking down. How was she still alive? How was she even conscious or breathing? Yet she was. The contrast between the frail scrap of her body and the burning, fierce determination of her mind. Her energy seemed to be centred there – as if her body had been cut away and then wasted away by slow starvation, the rampant multiplication of cancer cells and dehydration had taken over. But she hadn't lost her determination to be present and alert, so she could see me and engage with me.

I wanted to touch her but I instinctively knew to approach with caution. Here was Lizzy dying; here I was. She had changed, aged. Her face showed the torment of intense pain. I sat beside her bed as a visitor would, not too close.

We talked briefly about my journey from Wellington. A duck waddled across the courtyard outside the ranch sliders facing her bed. 'Those bloody ducks,' she gasped, 'filthy things.' I was shocked. To hear her irritation so near to death. This was no magnanimous embracing of all living things.

'This is my daughter Susan,' was how she introduced me to the hospice staff. It was the first time she ever said those words. They seemed gracious and wise. No doubt they had seen many death bed reconciliations.

I brought *The Writing Life* by Annie Dillard, a book I had sent her as a gift when I knew she wasn't well. I sat beside her. She was quiet, breathing, her eyes closed. 'Would you like me to read to you?' I asked.

'I can't bear it, I don't want you to comfort me,' she replied.

I was stung and almost tripped back as if touched by a force field at her refusal. This was her final work – to die on her own terms. Despite the ravage of the cancer and the pain she would grip hold of what little control she had left. She would face into it – the pain and death – and take no comfort in her journey. I wrote these notes in my journal at Lizzy's bedside:

Lizzy:	*Your tears are your strength. I want to be alone. No, I'm not scared of dying.*
Sue:	*Do you have a sense of spirit, of something greater than you?*
Lizzy:	*No*
Sue:	*Tino pai tou wairua koe / Your spirit is beautiful.*
Lizzy:	*When I came to Dunedin I wanted to cry all the time, I couldn't work out what was wrong. I went ballroom dancing and made friends then I talked to a friend who said, 'have you noticed what colour the people are? They're all white.'*

The small surge of energy that allowed her to be present for my arrival was suddenly gone. It must have taken her so much energy and will to climb out of her death dive to be present to me. Was that why she refused comfort? Because it would cause her to lose focus, to be distracted and maybe slip away while she was not on guard?

Eventually, she fell asleep. I took out *The Writing Life* and began to quietly read aloud. I hoped that hearing my voice would offer solace, even though she had refused it. After a half an hour, feeling shaken and overwhelmed, I left the room. I needed some kind of comfort. I imagined that to be in the form of a nicely rounded and bearded older chaplain – a kind of Santa Claus figure in my mind. Then by some miracle there he was walking towards me, the hospice chaplain. I almost fell into his arms. He led me to the sitting room at the end of the hall.

These spaces have a kind of resonance of all the people who have gone before, full of tears and dread and loss and sadness mixed in with comfort and kindness. Coming to this room was a reprieve after the high tension of Lizzy's room. It was a chance to step away from the face of death, the smell of death, the sound of death, the pain, the tubes.

When I returned, the door to Lizzy's room was closed and one of the staff asked me to wait outside in the corridor. I took a seat. Then I heard the most terrible wailing scream. It was a sound I had never heard before but I recognised it immediately to be a human in tortured pain. This continued for several minutes then ebbed to a whimper. People came and went from Lizzy's room, careful to close the door behind them.

Urgent movements and then silence. I sensed she wasn't dead. One of the nurses came out to me. She sat beside me and saw I was shaken. She told me Lizzy had acute anxiety. She didn't tell me what the anxiety was about exactly, but I could tell that it wasn't so much related to her impending death but rather about something she had carried with her for longer. Now, as she approached death, the normal controls against these emotions began to break down and the anxiety was rampaging.

'The pain is so bad that normal palliative relief won't touch it. Morphine won't work so we've given her heroin,' the nurse explained.

I guessed at that point there was no fear of addiction; they had to do whatever they could to make her physically comfortable. Some time had passed. I had to muster up the determination to go back to that room after her wailing and screaming had quieted down. When it seemed safe, I went back in. I sat down beside her and asked, 'How are you?'

'Exhausted,' she said. She wouldn't admit to the pain.

'There is so little left of you. I see you are determined to hold on to see Julie and Don,' I said.

'Yes,' she said, 'but I have more to do. I will not die until I have found a way to forgive myself.'

'To forgive yourself,' I asked, 'for what?'

'For giving you away.'

'I want you to know I have had a good life. I was adopted by good people who loved me. I'm not angry with you. I don't blame you for giving me up for adoption. I know you did what you had to do at the time.' I reached out gently, so gently, to touch her arm. She fell back, eyes closed, asleep.

In my memory, I see myself from a distance at her bedside, trying to reach across a vast chasm of time and pain and misunderstanding and damage; it is like looking at a ruin I cannot repair or restore. All I could hope was that by being there I could transmit through the ends of my warm fingers to her cold arm some small current of love to reassure her.

'It wasn't your fault. It wasn't terrible. You have not damaged me. I will be okay.'

I was, and still am, proud of how I responded to her that day. I tried to give her everything I wasn't able to in our first meeting, so many years before. She had taken the time to tell me the story of my birth, knowing she was the only person who could. She had borne witness to me coming into the world; I would bear witness to her leaving it.

One afternoon during my stay, Lizzy's friend Fiona came to visit. She brought a fresh energy into the room and a large tray of chocolates and strawberries, which were newly in season. It was strange to see these fruits of another world. Lizzy had stopped eating, but these were life-giving gifts.

Fiona came in her matter-of-fact way, with her tray of cheery strawberries, and brought us the positivity we needed. It felt as if she was visiting a friend who was on the road to recovery, not to death. I had the sense that she knew about me and she acted like my visit was a cause for celebration. It was the first time I realised that Lizzy had friends. Perhaps this was the one friend who she still allowed to see her.

As I had expected, my birth sister Julie was coming from London. The next day when I was sitting in Lizzy's room, Julie came in. Now, writing this, I can remember almost nothing about her – my sister who I had never met before this moment. I think she was attractive, but I can't even remember the colour of her hair. Lizzy told me that Julie had a son called Max. With no knowledge of the other, we had both named our sons Max. One Max was Lizzy's legitimate grandchild and the other, my Max, was acknowledged only in private letters.

The air was strained. The room had a vibration emanating from Lizzy who, from her deathbed, was still attempting to control the conversation and interactions. At the same time, I sensed a yearning for us to take control – to take it away from her – the burden of managing these gaps in our relationships. But she wasn't ready to let go, and Julie and I weren't ready to take it. Julie wasn't sure what to do with me, but she acknowledged that I had some right to be there.

She told me that her brother Don, my birth brother, was coming back from Australia and that he did not want to see me. It was a strange passivity I adopted. Her words numbed and shocked me but I accepted her authority as the 'big sister'. I was the older sister, the first born, but in that family dynamic she had stepped in to take control of the relationships and to do what she thought would protect her family. How strange to realise, how shocking for me to realise, she was protecting her family from me. This strange dynamic of Lizzy wanting to tell the truth about me, to own me as her child to the staff and to her friend, yet when her family arrived she wasn't able to hold that connection. I was an awkward intruder, a difficult problem to be managed.

I waited in one of the sitting rooms for visitors that looked out toward the stream and trees. The door was slightly open and I saw along the corridor a man who must have been my brother Don walking towards Lizzy's room. He was tall with dark hair and had a strong physical presence. Then someone closed the door.

I sat with my head in my hands, knowing that along the corridor in Lizzy's room there was a sad family reunion. Knowing too that they were aware of my presence like a dark brooding energy, scared that I might choose to come in and make myself visible, hoping I wouldn't, willing me to stay away, to remain invisible.

I did what I was told, then eventually I left the hospice and went back to the strange little motel where I was staying, a plastic inflatable man waving outside. The owners at the motel were warm and friendly. I had told them that my mother was dying in the hospice, but added none of the details.

I went into my room, made a cup of tea, and sat down on the bed sobbing. I remember the sound of the jug boiling and the damp smell of the concrete block motel room. That plain room became my place of safety, away from the trauma and rejection at the hospice.

There was a radio interview I once heard with the Scottish Poet Laureate, talking about going to her birth mother's funeral and telling no one who she was or why she was there. The interviewer, Kim Hill, asked her, 'Why didn't you tell the truth?' She responded, 'I don't know, I played along with the lie. I accepted my place as an outsider.'

Looking back now, I see my passivity and compliance. These are not adjectives people would use normally to describe me. I understand this is what happens in shock and trauma – people can become mute and silenced. How we go along with abuse and injustice, how we collude with the ways that others damage us.

I get angry and frustrated seeing others, especially women, passively accepting a place they have been assigned to by their family or in the world of work because they are women. It's not personal; it's socialised behaviour. I want them to rage against it. I want them to fight back, to raise their voices. Yet here was I, relegated to the corner, only just tolerated, and I too went along with it.

CHAPTER NINE

Go Well and Be Happy

One morning in early January I turned on my cell phone to clear my messages and there was one from the hospice asking me to call. I knew immediately. They told me that Lizzy died the night before, Monday 10 January 2005, about 10.30 pm.

I was with Max at the motel at Te Anau after a holiday in the Catlins with friends. I didn't stop to process or think. Max and I drove to Queenstown as we had planned. But it all felt wrong. I felt grumpy, tired, and sick of travelling and sleeping in new places.

The next day Max and I were biking along the Franklin track when Julie rang to say that they didn't want me to come to the funeral. Don wouldn't come if I was there.

'I'm not asking you. I'm telling you. We do not want you there. I will make a big scene if I have to stop you at the door. We will have you arrested if you come. There is no way I'm going to ruin this for my brother,' Julie told me.

I replied, 'I see it differently. I'm not ruining it for Don. I want to come to the funeral to say goodbye to Lizzy. How am I supposed to grieve? I'll take some time to think about what you've said and get back to you. Thank you for being honest about how you feel.'

I called Brian, the hospice chaplain, to ask his advice. He suggested attending the gravesite when the funeral was over. I also spoke to my dear friend Jude. She suggested I didn't go, it would be too hard emotionally. I conceived the idea of holding my own memorial service in Wellington.

Julie phoned again the next day while Max and I were driving and I told her I had decided not to attend.

'Thank you for that.' she said, 'We really appreciate it.'

That gate, which had been tentatively swinging without Lizzy standing guard, suddenly slammed in my face. This was not my family. I was not welcome. It was as though the years of work spent to bring Lizzy the peace and the connection she needed were now just another shameful secret to bury. Another relationship left to be forgotten and erased.

Max and I finished our holiday together. I did my best to be present, promising myself there would be time to grieve properly at some later point in time.

A few weeks after I returned home, I was surprised to find a richly textured white envelope from the Blue Lizzy Museum Collection had arrived in the mail. It was Lizzy's last letter.

There was no date on the letter but I assume from the clear, vibrantly sloping cursive that it was written before she became very unwell, before her mind had been clouded by pain medications. I imagined her putting things in order at her home in Highgate, Dunedin. The little white cottage surrounded by her beloved lilies and white roses.

The letter was on matching paper with three blue bowls in the top left hand and an abstract image of a blue flower in the bottom right. She had chosen the stationery carefully. There she was in my mind, sitting down to write the letter she planned to have sent by her lawyer after her death. I admired her intention to send me her final words, to ensure I heard from her one last time. It was a simple message.

Dear Sue,
You have been loved,
You are loved now
And if there is any kind of afterlife, you will continue to be loved.

Thank you for coming into my life on two counts –
at birth and as an adult.
Go well and be happy

My love,
Lizzy

She underlined the word 'be' as if it was a command – you will go on and be happy. I remember she often said it like that when we talked. It was like she could see straight inside of me, knowing I didn't typically see myself as a happy person. In her final words to me, as she was preparing to die, she wanted me to try. The letter is simple, but it says everything. I imagine what I would say to Max in a final letter, and it's not far off from Lizzy's. Be happy.

In later years, I would become a detective to my own story, piecing together the history of my own life, my heritage through government agencies, blood tests, archived records. Like my Scottish detective great-grandfather, I would compile the facts in pursuit of a lost narrative.

A year later, around Easter time, I decided to visit Dunedin again. I went down with my friend Diana to cycle the Otago Rail Trail. But our final destination would take us to Lizzy's grave, the location of the funeral I never attended. I was looking for closure, and this trip was my pilgrimage to memorialise Lizzy, to say the proper goodbye that I had been refused before. My memory around this time has become rather sketchy, so I asked Diana what she remembered from the trip. We talked at a cheap Malaysian restaurant on Cuba Street in Wellington, one of the old haunts from our student days. I started the voice memo app on my phone and asked her to hold it close while she told the story.

We were the last group through the Otago Rail Trail before the end of the season, and it was bitterly cold. The cycle trip ended on a low. I had hypothermia, and ended up in Naseby Hospital. Addison's disease left me particularly susceptible to health issues like this, but after a 100 mg hydrocortisone injection and a day surrounded by hot water bottles, I recovered enough to leave. The cycle trail ended in Dunedin and we had planned to stay two nights. Diana remembered that I was still very raw from Lizzy's death, still feeling the rejection of not being invited to the funeral. I wanted to find her grave. It was a beautiful day in Dunedin so we caught a taxi to the cemetery at Anderson's Bay on the South side of the Peninsula. It was a beautiful place with views overlooking the ocean.

We had no idea where Lizzy's headstone was, so we wandered around the large graveyard, hoping we would stumble upon her.

Unsuccessful, we went to the large concrete crematorium at the entrance to the cemetery. There, we were given a record of Elizabeth Mackenzie, aged sixty-three years who died on 10 January 2005. We were told she had been cremated. No grave. The Dunedin City Council grave service produced this record:

Type of Service: None
Ashes Disposal Return to Funeral Director 15 January 2005

No service? That seemed odd, given that Julie had asked me not to go to the funeral. Perhaps it was such a small gathering with no formal process that it did not constitute a funeral. In the empty crematorium, we sat on long wooden pews, the view out to Anderson's Bay and the velvet curtains at the front of the room. I walked up and looked behind the curtain to find a type of conveyor belt where the casket was placed on - presumably leading to an oven.

I sat in the pew and tried to imagine the scene of her funeral, but I couldn't. I couldn't imagine and I couldn't feel anything but a sense of numbness. Diana remembers me weeping silently, coming to terms with the fact that this pilgrimage wasn't going to finish as I hoped.

'You were desperate,' she told me at that Malaysian restaurant. 'You'd built up this hope in your mind. As your friend, I so wanted you to be able to find her. But it wasn't what you hoped for. It was like she had been erased.'

I wasn't going to find anything. It was as if Lizzy had evaporated, all trace of her gone, up in smoke, with not even a grave to mark her existence.

We decided to go to the Hope Brothers Funeral Home, listed as the funeral director, and see if we could find something there. It was a funny old fashioned place, a red brick building. The funeral director on duty was wary when I told him the story and why I was searching for information about Lizzy. I assumed he had been told about me, maybe even given instructions not to release any information. Eventually, he told me it was a secular funeral with no celebrant and only ten to twelve people in attendance. He didn't know where her ashes were scattered.

I realised then that the service likely wasn't held at the crematorium at all, but here, at this funeral home. I tried again to picture it. Just a handful of people – it really was just a private family service. Perhaps that was what she had wanted. Something isolated, protected in some way. This idea of a private funeral was foreign to me. In my family growing up, everyone was welcome. Everyone was there to celebrate, to remember. But this family put privacy above all else. How strange it would have been if I had been invited, one of only ten there to memorialise Lizzy's life. There would have been no hiding in the back at a funeral like that. I would have been an awkward intruder into the privacy of another family. A family I wasn't part of.

The final journey we made was to the cottage in Highgate, where Lizzy lived before hospice. This was where she had written many of her letters to me, describing the renovations and her beautiful cottage garden. We couldn't knock on the door; we were only observers. There was a rosebush near the front garden, and Diana remembered me picking a single flower.

'That was as close as you got to finding something tangible. Otherwise, there was nothing,' she said.

CHAPTER TEN

Finding Cynthia Winters

'Ko te maumahara kore ki ngā whakapapa o ōu mātua tīpuna, e rite ana ki te
pūkaki awa kāore ōna hikuawa, ki te rākau rānei kāore ōna pakiaka.

To forget one's ancestors is to be a brook without a source, a tree without its roots.

Aroha, Dr Hinemoa Elder

Seventeen years passed after Lizzy's death before I returned to the story of my origins. In this time, I had moved to Waiheke Island, and started my own business as a director and consultant for women leaders. I spent most of my days advocating for gender diversity in leadership, standing on boards for housing accessibility, and in my free time, travelling, cycling, swimming, and spending time with friends across the country.

Max had established his life and his career in Wellington. He was thirty when the pandemic started, and I was sixty, nearing the age Lizzy had been when I saw her for the last time. The weather inside of me had shifted, and there awakened a pull towards that box I had carefully kept stowed away since 2005.

Most years, the forces that kept the lid closed had been stronger than my desire to open it. I had sometimes acknowledged the feeling but so far had distracted myself with end of year busyness and Christmas holiday preparations. But in a hundred days of COVID lockdown, a month before Christmas of 2021, something shifted – a new, and far more urgent determination.

There, at the brink of this new effort, stood the threshold guardians, alert with their swords crossed in front of my uncovered stories. I forced myself to write anyway. I would see them not as demi-gods trying to keep me away, but instead imagined them protecting something precious, almost sacred.

This part of my journey started with the tangible. The letters, all laid out on the long trestle table. I wanted facts. Truths. Evidence to fill the gaps of half-told and half-remembered stories.

My first channel of enquiry: Adoption Services at the government agency Oranga Tamariki, named the Department of Social Welfare at the time of my adoption. I sent through the official form, the *Request for Pre-Adoptive New Zealand Birth Certificate*. I provided my details, my current name, and then there was a box titled:

> Name at birth (if different from above). Note this is your name before you were adopted if you know that.

This unsettled me. It implied that some adopted children were given a name at birth. The boxes said 'surname at birth' and 'first names at birth'. I wondered if Lizzy had named me, had given me her surname Winters despite knowing it would be changed days later.

The request form stated that if you were adopted before 1 March 1986 you must receive counselling from a social worker or approved person or organisation. The Register of Births, Deaths and Marriages will post your pre-adoptive birth Certificate and contact details to your chosen counsellor and they will then give you your Certificate.

A list of counsellors was provided as required by the Adult Adoption Information Act 1985. For the District of Auckland there were two choices, a senior practitioner social worker at Oranga Tamariki and then the names of three independent counsellors, all women. I called the first one, Alison, thinking it was better to find a private counsellor who may be more responsive. Only her landline was listed. I called but there was no response.

Impatient now that I had decided to act, I dialled the Senior Practitioner Social Worker Adoption Services Auckland Region. A woman answered, sounding frail and faraway at 10 am on a Monday, introducing herself as

Lynne. My first instinct was to make an excuse and end the call, doubting that she would be able to help me or would be even interested in doing so. I asked a couple of questions to test her response and she seemed to know how the process worked. She asked me for some details, so I told her my name, sensing that I could trust her. She said she could help me and that she may be able to start the search process which can be protracted and lengthy while I filled in the form and wait for it to find its way to Wellington through the bureaucracy of Births, Deaths and Marriages. She could then start the process of requesting the records of my adoption held in the government archives.

She asked me, 'What was the name of your birth mother?' I started to speak, I hesitated and the tears came and I could barely speak her name. Lynne was quiet, listening, holding a space for me to speak the words, to voice the sacred name of my now dead mother.

I started again. 'Lizzy Mackenzie, or Elizabeth Mackenzie,' I said, then remembered that Mackenzie was her married name. Her name at the time of my birth was Winters, her family name. 'Elizabeth Winters,' I corrected, 'but I can't remember her middle name.'

Lynne then asked me the name of my adoptive parents. Those came naturally to my mind, but just as I said them, 'Cecily Watson and Peter Watson,' the tears came again.

I learned that sometimes there is very little in the adoption records, no reasons given for why a child was assigned to a particular pair of adopted parents. Sometimes, it was as simple as the colour of their hair or other physical characteristics, level of education or religious background. There may also be a record from the Child Welfare division, a report about the parents and case notes.

I felt that sense again that the guardians had opened a gate and Lynne was inside waiting to meet me. I had found the right person at the right time. It was as if the road had risen up to meet me, and this time I had someone to hold me as I walked towards it.

A month later, two days before Christmas, I received an email from Lynne:

Dear Sue,

Please find attached, as requested, historical non-identifying information on your birth: parents and identifying details for your birth mother. Details regarding your birth and adoption are also included.

Please bear in mind the following in relation to the historical information provided from the Department of Education, Child Welfare Division adoption records and Fairleigh Hospital,

Motherhood of Man record cards:

The non-identifying information on your birth parents has been transcribed from a departmental report dated 26 June 1962 and undated Fairleigh Hospital record cards.

This information was recorded in good faith, and we cannot vouch for its accuracy.

There could prove to be discrepancies between this and other sources of information.

Your birth parents' details appear to have been gathered only from your birth mother.

We have been obliged to consider the privacy of your birth parents in releasing their non-identifying information to you, and this information has been released to you as a transcribed summary in accordance with our current policy.

I hope that this is of assistance. Please don't hesitate to contact me if you wish to discuss any aspect of this.

Lynne
Adoption Service, Oranga Tamariki- Ministry for Children

Attached were transcribed summaries regarding my birth and adoption history, all taken from the Child Welfare Division of the Department of

Adoption Records, Fairleigh Hospital and Motherhood of Man record cards. Motherhood of Man, the organisation that supported Lizzy before the birth, caught my attention. I had never heard of this place and made a mental note to do some research after digesting this new information.

It was clearly not all of the information available. Lynne had decided what was legal and appropriate to pass on to me – weighing up the privacy protections of my birth mother against my right to know information about my origins. The information is given 'in confidence,' effectively preventing me from disclosing these details to anyone else. It is why I have changed the name and identifying details of my birth mother and everyone else mentioned, hoping this will be enough to ensure no one can be identified. It was a struggle to disguise my own history, but of course, I was legally required to anonymise everything I wrote.

The transcribed summary included in Lynne's letter began with my birth details and my birth mother's details.

IN-CONFIDENCE

Susan Anne Watson

Details on your birth, birth family and adoption
Sources: Child Welfare Division, Department of Education
Adoption Records Fairleigh Hospital, Motherhood of Man
Record Cards

Your birth details:

Due:	*27 September 1962*
Born:	*31 October 1962*
Born at:	*Fairleigh Hospital, Grey Lynn, Auckland*
Birth:	*Normal, lungs clear*
Birth weight:	*6lbs 14oz*
Birth registered:	*7 November 1962*

Your birth mother's details:

Name:	*As recorded on your pre-adoptive birth certificate*
Temporary address:	▨ *Mangere, Auckland*
Normal home address:	▨ *, Hastings*
Age/date of birth:	*20 years old; born 25 December 1941*
Religion:	*Church of England*
Ethnicity:	*European*
Marital status:	*Single*
Education:	*2 years secondary education – commercial course. Left school at 15, at Form 5 level.*
Adult education:	*Shorthand typing, English.*
Occupation:	*Student Nurse; may complete her nursing training.*
Health:	*Good personal and family health, except that your maternal birth grandmother had hay fever.*
Interests:	*Basketball, swimming. Fashion. Had done a great deal of singing. Had been busy studying.*
Physical description:	*5' 5 ½", medium build. fair, hazel eyes, fairish skin.*
Family situation:	*Our records note that your maternal birth grandparents were unaware that your birth mother was pregnant with you.*

There it was. Information I had waited decades to find. The only information the State would give me about my birth and adoption was a transcribed summary with a note that they could not vouch for its accuracy. I found it hard to focus and absorb this flood of information after such a long silence. I read it over and over, noticing new details each time.

My immediate response was to look for similarities and differences between Lizzy and me. We both liked swimming, singing and studying, but I didn't share her interest in basketball or fashion. Her religion was listed as Church of England, the same denomination in which I was raised.

I noted she had only two years of secondary schooling, studying commercial subjects and had left school in the fifth form. I thought of my own schooling experience at Auckland Girls' Grammar in the 'A' stream towards accredited University Entrance, and how we looked down on the 'commercial girls' who were taught literally in the lower level of the school. I wondered why she left school so early? Her father would have left the family by then, and I wondered if she was escaping an unhappy home life. As she had told me, she was studying to be a nurse in Wellington when she became pregnant. The record noted that her parents were unaware that Lizzy was pregnant, yet I discovered in the paperwork that she recorded her mother's address as her home.

The record noted that Lizzy 'may complete her nursing training,' but of course she never did. Instead, she married Don a few months later and started a legitimate family. After her marriage dissolved, she went to University to study Psychology, eventually qualifying as a Clinical Psychologist. I realised then how important that degree must have been for her after several unfinished educational attempts in the past.

My due date also caught my attention. I was born thirty four days late at Fairleigh hospital in Grey Lynn Auckland. But how was my due date determined? Did Lizzy know the date of my conception or was it an educated guess by a midwife or doctor? I was a healthy baby weighing almost seven pounds, born to a healthy mother. Seven days later my birth was registered and approval was given for my adoption placement.

The details about Lizzy were recorded in June, four months before my birth and five months into her pregnancy. I calculated that I was conceived in the summer of 1962, sometime in February.

In the same paper, Lizzy had also filled out my 'alleged' birth father's details. As Lynne had noted, 'There could prove to be discrepancies between this and other sources of information.'

Your alleged birth father's details (as of 26 June 1962):

Name:	*Not named on Child Welfare Division adoption records and Motherhood of Man record cards*
Age:	*25 years old*
Ethnicity/Nationality:	*Full European, Greek. Had been in New Zealand for 11 years.*
Education:	*University Entrance; had been to university for 2 years (accountancy). Left at 20.*
Occupation:	*Taxi Driver*
Health:	*Good health. Had worn glasses since he was 11 years old. Family health good as far as known.*
Interests:	*Not interested in sport*
Description:	*Very New Zealand in appearance and outlook. Medium build. Dark hair, brown eyes, olive skin.*

When Lizzy gave accounts to me in the past about the two men who could have been my father, they often felt deliberately confusing. Here, three months before my birth, she provided convincing details about David's identity without actually naming him.

She obviously knew him well enough to give details like the length of time he had been in New Zealand and that he had been wearing glasses since he was eleven. I assume this was not a 'one-night stand,' but a boyfriend.

An image formed of a Greek man with dark hair, brown eyes and olive skin yet also, as she noted, very 'New Zealand in appearance and outlook,' as though she was making it clear that the baby would be unequivocally white. I knew that it was not uncommon for birth mothers to deliberately provide incorrect information about the father of their baby either to protect the men or to give their baby a better chance of adoption. Leaving out or adding details to increase the desirability of the baby was a way to increase the chances of getting in with a 'good' adoption couple.

I wonder if Lizzy had stressed David's 'New Zealand appearance and outlook' to try to offer me the best chance of getting a White, middle-class New Zealand family. She noted that David had completed two years of university study, a way for her to indicate that he was intelligent and capable, details that may have made me a more desirable baby.

Rather than listing out his interests and skills, Lizzy only said that he wasn't interested in sport. It was an odd detail to include, and I wondered if that trait of his was something she didn't like, something that she would have remembered clearly.

He was five years older than her and had only moved to New Zealand at age fourteen. I assumed English wasn't his first language, but he still managed to gain University Entrance for accountancy. By the time Lizzy met him, she said he was a taxi driver. I was immediately doubtful about this detail and wondered if it was something she made up to give the impression that he would be unable to afford to support her and the baby, somehow a grasp for justification of her choice to adopt.

In the same package of information, Lynne included information about the Motherhood of Man Movement, the incorporated society that operated the private maternity hospital and day nursery called Fairleigh where I was born.

> The objectives of the Movement were the welfare, the protection of expectant mothers – married and unmarried – and the provision, where necessary, of medical and associated advice and assistance to destitute or deserted wives, widows and working mothers.

The Society ran a private maternity hospital and eventually a day nursery. The record noted that, 'funds were raised by membership fees, donation tins placed in shops and businesses, fairs, raffles, rag collections, fashion parades, sewing bees, Community Chest, and the unmarried Social Security money paid over while hospitalised.' They continued to run the hospital and arrange adoptions until their closure in 1981.

> A bit more digging about Motherhood of Man produced a fascinating article from Anne Else, *The Need is Ever Present: The Motherhood of Man and Stranger Adoption in New Zealand*, published by the Stout Research Center at Victoria University in 1989.

As a researcher myself it was strange to find an academic article so close to my own history. I noted her use of the term 'stranger' adoption, not the more sanitised 'closed adoption' term I have always used. She describes the system of adoption in the Pākehā legal system in New Zealand, the first country in the British Empire to pass an Adoption Act in 1881. From that time until 1980, 103,000 adoptions took place. The Motherhood of Man was, 'the principal private, non-denominational agency offering assistance to unmarried mothers and placing children for adoption in Auckland after the Second World War' (p. 47).

The Motherhood of Man, Else argued, 'focused on the baby; in their view, placing it in a home where it was wanted solved not only the mother's problem but also met the needs of a childless couple. They quickly came to see adoption as best for everyone concerned, and operated on that assumption' (p. 48). The deal was based on the birth mothers agreeing to the adoption and to never seeing the baby again. Motherhood of Man also operated their own private maternity hospital. This enabled them to expand their offering to unwed mothers. They offered maternity services at Fairleigh Hospital to married mothers at cost while five rooms were specifically allocated to unwed mothers.[2]

In an effort to prepare the unwed mothers for the responsibilities of motherhood and presumably to make it easier for them to choose to adopt, some had access to the opportunity to live in a 'safely distant family, usually in return for household help. Often other clergy or doctors took

---

2 Cussen, Lone. "Children First: The Motherhood of Man Movement and single motherhood in 1940s and 1950s New Zealand." *Records of the Auckland Museum* 52. Auckland War Memorial Museum, 2017.

them in; there was a network of such exchanges across the country' (Else, p. 53). Lizzy gave Māngere as her temporary address in this paperwork. She had told me once that she stayed with a doctor and his wife and worked for them in exchange for board. I concluded that Lizzy would have moved up to Auckland, where she didn't know anyone, before she began to 'show' and was billeted to a doctor and his wife through Motherhood of Man. I assume they lived at the address in Māngere given in my pre-adoptive birth records.

Evidence of baby-farming at the Motherhood of Man (charging fees for adoption), financial irregularities and lack of assistance to unmarried mothers who wished to keep their children led to the investigation by the Government of the Motherhood of Man and other similar institutions in the early 1950s. The Adoption Bill in 1954 was drafted with a long submission from the Motherhood of Man.

> Secrecy was a major concern. Motherhood of Man believed there should be no possible opportunity for the natural mother to learn the adoptive parents' identity...Citing anecdotal evidence, it raised the bogey of the mother finding out where her child was, and making a nuisance of herself; or worse, blackmailing the adoptive parents (ibid., p. 60).

The Adoption Act was passed in 1955 and remained in place until partially amended by the Adult Adoption Information Act in 1985, opening the door to birth mothers and adopted babies to request information about each other but also for either party to deny access to that information.

By 1961, the year before my birth, there was a greater supply of babies than prospective adoptive parents. The baby market had become unbalanced, as Else explains would-be parents were:

> eagerly welcomed and could, to some extent, specify the sort of child they wanted. A 'grading' system quickly emerged, according to a child's sex, health, race, religious affiliation, and (to a lesser extent) family background. The most easily placed babies, perfect Pākehā girls, rose to the top of the list,

and boys who were disabled and/or of mixed race sank to the bottom' (ibid., p. 48).

So it really was a lottery – a lottery that I won by being born a 'perfect Pākehā girl.' Reinforced, or at least not undermined, by the details Lizzy provided of my 'very New Zealand in appearance and outlook' birth father.

Applicants for adoption were asked to provide their full names, occupation, religion and, 'some idea of your colouring is helpful' (ibid., p. 55). Mum and Dad, a middle class Pākehā couple, had the 'pick of babies' and I assume they picked me.

Finally, Lynne had transcribed some details of my adoption placement that start on the day of my birth and end eight months later with the final adoption order, the date at which the State formally ended its oversight of my adoption.

Your adoption placement:

31 October 1962   *The Child Welfare Division was notified of your birth.*

7 November 1962   *The Motherhood of Man Agency received the Child Welfare*
Division approval for your adoption placement. This is a legal requirement.

12 November 1962
You were placed with your adoptive parents and were making good progress. This placement was arranged by an agency called the Motherhood of Man. The Child Welfare Division was advised of your discharge from Fairleigh Hospital. Our records indicate that your birth mother felt that an adoption placement was best for you. You were making good progress under Plunket supervision.

6 December 1962   *Interim Adoption Order, New Plymouth Court.*

30 January 1963	*You were well.*
14 March 1963	*You were contented and well.*
20 May 1963	*You had had the flu but were*
	otherwise doing very well.
21 May 1963	*You were making excellent progress. You were an attractive and happy baby. You were a dearly loved member of a happy family.*
21 June 1963	*Final Adoption Order, New Plymouth Court*

Lizzy was vulnerable and therefore so was I. If, as Lizzy told me, I was taken away from her as soon as I was born, then I spent the first twelve days of my life in a nursery at Fairleigh hospital dependent on the charity of well-meaning people who had set up the Motherhood of Man to cater for mothers and babies in precarious circumstances. If Lizzy left the maternity hospital soon after my birth that means I was an orphan for twelve days and technically so in law until my adoption was confirmed eight months later.

As someone who is now a professional director on the boards of charitable organisations set up to provide housing and care for people in vulnerable circumstances in Auckland, it is strange and humbling to think of myself as once being the recipient of charity. To know that I was once dependent on the good will of strangers at a time of total vulnerability shifts my sense of self. I have always thought of myself as blessed to be cared for and then adopted safely into a family where I was loved and given a good, very good, childhood. And I think that is true. What I hadn't accounted for was my pre-adoption story as an orphan, a reality that no doubt the state sanctioned narrative of the happy adopted child and parents was designed to erase.

I realised that in being adopted I was literally 'reclassified' from being an orphan who was the illegitimate child of an unmarried, 'destitute'

European mother, (presumably) pregnant to a Greek immigrant taxi driver, to being the youngest daughter of a married, middle class, Anglican European couple. I was grateful for this transformation and the childhood, family, and access to opportunities that I was given as a result.

The interim adoption order was made three weeks prior to Christmas and three months later I was described as being 'contented and well.' How happy and relieved Mum must have been with that assessment as the interim adoption order remained in place until at least six months, 6 June 1963. Custody of 'the child' was only given after that time and I assume it would be revoked if Child Welfare were not satisfied with the placement. It was just about the perfect report a new parent could hope for, and Mum would not have taken this for granted. I know she would have prepared well, and taken every opportunity to show the inspector that I was a good and a happy baby.

Six months later, Mum and Dad could apply for an adoption order. If they did not do so by 6 December 1963 the interim order stated that 'you may lose custody of the child.' I noted that the custody order was made on 21 June 1963, soon after they were eligible to do so. By 21 May 1963 I was described as making 'excellent progress' and as, 'an attractive and happy baby. You were a dearly loved member of a happy family.' And so I was.

Written on the side of my newly-acquired pre-adoption form, I noticed the confirmation of the completed adoption order, running along the right hand side of the file. I realised that the next piece of the puzzle was something I had already found. The year before, after my father Peter passed away, I found two documents in a brown manila folder. Dad's writing at the top of the folder simply said "SUSAN." In it was the Interim Order and the Final Order of Adoption.

'Notice of Interim Order' from the Magistrate's Court held at New Plymouth.

In the Matter of the Adoption Act, 1955 and in the matter of an application by Peter Ronald Watson and Cicely Edith Watson to adopt a child.

To Peter Ronald Watson of New Plymouth, Company Manager and Cicely Edith Watson his wife on 6th December 1962 the Court made an order in relation to your application to adopt a child. The order was an interim order only as required by the Adoption Act 1955, and while it remains in force the following conditions apply:

You are entitled to the custody of the child
Any Child Welfare Officer may, at all reasonable times, visit and enter the residence in which the child is living:
  The child is not to be taken out of New Zealand without the leave of the Court:
  You must give to a Child Welfare Officer at least seven days' notice before changing your residence: provided that where an emergency makes any immediate change necessary it will be sufficient if you give notice within forty-eight hours after leaving your previous residence.
  The Interim order is not an adoption order. An adoption order cannot be obtained until a further application has been made after six months. The application to the Court for the issue of the adoption order may be made after 6 June 1963, if the child has been continuously in your care for not less than [blank] since the date on which the interim order was made or since such earlier date (if any) as the placing or keeping of the child in your home for the purpose of adoption was approved by a Child Welfare Officer.

The application to the Court for the adoption order must be made before the 6th December 1963. The interim order will lapse on that date. If you do not apply in time you may lose custody of the child.

Stapled to the front of the Notice of Interim Order is a smaller sheet of paper on letterhead from a solicitor in New Plymouth. It is addressed to P.R. Watson in Lower Hutt and dated 26 June 1963.

Dear Peter,

We wish to confirm that the adoption order was made in respect of Susan on the 21st June.

In just a half page of text, I had been given a new life under new ownership. Simple, done and dusted, signed and dated. It was less administrative paperwork than what would be required to buy a house, or even a car.

The final piece of information about my origins arrived by mail, my pre-adoptive New Zealand Birth Certificate. A single sheet of thick light-yellow official looking paper. The record begins:

| First/given name(s) | Cynthia |
| Surname/family name | Winters |

I said it aloud – *Cynthia Winters*. It sounded so strange, foreign in my mouth. Cynthia Winters. It was cold, biting, filled with harsh consonants, forcing me to bite into the syllables to get them out.

This name wasn't mine. It didn't feel like me, yet here it was, probably one of the first sounds I had heard spoken to me in my life. Cynthia Winters. It felt strange and wrong, more uncomfortable every time I repeated it.

I wondered where the name had come from. The surname I recognised as Lizzy's, and felt the oddness of passing down a family name for a child who had already been put up for adoption. The first name didn't feel in any way familiar. My immediate thoughts rushed to family members, thinking maybe Lizzy had named me after an aunt or great-grandmother or perhaps a good friend from her childhood. Or maybe it had been in her mind recently – another woman she met at Motherhood of Man, a nurse, or an expecting mother. It shocked me that Lizzy had heard this name and liked it so much to pass it along to a daughter. It felt entirely old fashioned and dusty. Certainly, a name I was pleased I did not keep.

Then I realised that this was likely the name Lizzy had held onto for twenty-six years, imagining her baby Cynthia growing up in the world. Perhaps I lived in her mind as Cynthia until I responded to her very first letter. She never told me about this name, though. She never mentioned what she thought all those years, or who she imagined when she pictured her adopted child.

It was clear that Cynthia was not just a name I had lost; she was a part of me. Cynthia the orphan. Susan the adopted child. Cynthia the unwanted child of Lizzy. Susan the 'chosen' and perfect daughter of Cicely. Cynthia was abandoned. Susan was adored.

I realised that I still carried Cynthia with me, ignoring her, pushing her away. But the time had come to see her. I needed to learn to love Cynthia, to hold her and accept her. I could not abandon her now that I had finally found her again. She had been waiting for so long to be remembered, to be embraced, to become unified with Susan at last. Lizzy had come looking for me, to finish her story. Now, I had found Cynthia, and it was time to finish our story.

CHAPTER ELEVEN

A Mother Shared

I was on a roll. My investigation was turning up clues everywhere I looked. With my official adoption records, I had an image of the first few days of my life. But what about the motherhood I had never experienced with Lizzy? Harnessing my newfound focus on solving the mysteries of my own life, I decided to contact my birth sister again. All I could remember about Julie was that she was younger than me, and that we shared a birth mother and possibly a birth father too. It had been sixteen years since she had called to tell me not to come to Lizzy's funeral.

I found her profile on LinkedIn. Her photo was instantly recognisable. A younger version of Lizzy with the same long slim face and fine straight hair. I sent a short introductory email to test the waters, and checked a couple of times a day for a reply. It was November, and I wondered if the time of year brought back memories of Lizzy's death, as it did for me. My hope was that this time of year would, consciously or not, awaken some pull towards the past that might make it easier for her to connect with me.

Ten days later, she responded:

Hi Sue, In regard to your message, I've spoken with my brother and we're happy to provide what information we can but please be aware mum's parents separated when mum was young and her mum was not a great communicator when it came to family history so we don't have lots of info (and the father was never on the scene from what we can tell). Let me know what you're ideally after and I will pass on what we have.

There was so much revelation in these two short sentences, yet I was only left hungry for more. She had spoken with her brother Don. They agreed to share family information. Even another clue about Lizzy's father – my grandfather, Harold, who 'was never on the scene' after he returned from war and left the family. In just a paragraph, Julie sent my mind pinging, hopeful and excited by this newfound tap of knowledge.

I wondered about that comment about Lizzy's mother not communicating well. She was setting my expectations, forecasting the dead ends in my search. Images of Lizzy's story about her uncles being killed in the war on the day of her birth and her father's alcoholism came to mind, mixed with descriptions from her letters about the sadness and shame her mother had faced. Perhaps Julie knew more about these fragments; perhaps she didn't.

Her message was crystal clear, and her tone almost business-like. It was apparent that she would help me out of obligation – but she wasn't here to get to know me, to welcome me. I had knocked on her door, and she had cracked it open. No invitation for a cup of tea, but she would tell me what I needed to know. A direct approach might have been what she needed to feel safe, to know our relationship was that of a librarian and a patron. Strictly about passing on information, knowledge, facts – and nothing more. I was thankful just to get a response. Matching the tone to show I understood, I replied right away.

> *I don't know much either but a good place to start would be if you can tell me the full name of Lizzy's father and mother and their approximate date of birth and place of birth. I remember Lizzy telling me that she didn't know her father well. I think she told me her grandfather or great grandfather emigrated from the UK but not sure if that was on her mother or father's side?*

Julie replied two days later, filled with answers for me. *Attached is all we have on mum's family.* Then, a flood of information. She had gone to the trouble of scanning letters and documents that Lizzy had sent her over the years. New pieces to the puzzle, new documents, photos, scraps of truth to fit into the tapestry of this story I was discovering. I read them over and over to absorb every detail.

You'll see letters from mum asking for help tracking down her grandfather – at one point she was thinking of applying for a visa to live in the UK and needed this info for it.

I realised that Lizzy likely had her own white cardboard box. She had walked this path at some point, trying to capture her own history for her own reasons. Julie included the documents that Lizzy had tried to transcribe for readability, almost as if she knew someone, someday might actually want to read them.

Julie went on to tell me what she knew about her grandfather, our grandfather, Harold Winters.

We were told he died from war wounds after returning from the war but years later the next line was that he died when mum was pregnant with me (c1964). He was never buried and about 35 years later a cousin claimed his ashes and got a plot for him. The story goes that no one in the family wanted anything to do with him, so he was literally left on the shelf at the crematorium!

If I find anything else will pass on but nana was not the warmest character and I expect threw away everything to do with Harold and it seems her dad could have been an alcoholic so expect that wasn't much fun.

Julie seemed to have found these two conflicting accounts of Harold's death in letters from Lizzy. Lizzy's children were told that he died from war injuries, a rather heroic, honourable way to go. But it clearly wasn't the truth, if his death certificate recorded that he died in the mid-sixties. At one point, Lizzy had told me vaguely that her dad had returned home needing hospital and home care. Soon after, she said, her parents' relationship crumbled and he ended up leaving the family. The truth had been obscured.

I wasn't the only one who hadn't been given a straight answer about my history. Julie was also left with fragments and details about her own heritage, too. Harold didn't die after the war – but instead had done something horrible, something that made his family ashamed. Maybe he was convicted of a crime, or his alcoholism was that bad, or his choice to leave had left the family in ruins; I never did uncover the source of his shame. And when he did finally pass away, he was left unacknowledged for thirty-five years, until his son eventually claimed and buried his ashes in the town where his family had lived. Julie relayed in her email that she had no idea where Roy, her uncle, was or if he was even alive.

The Winters confounded me; for generations, they lied to one another to cover up unbearable truths. The year of 1964 would have been a tumultuous year for Lizzy. She was pregnant, not two years after giving me up for adoption, and then she lost her estranged father, the person she once told me she adored, but also who had clearly damaged his family enough to be erased.

The level of complication she must have felt during that time would have been a huge weight to bear. She would have been privately, secretly grieving. No funeral, no support, and surely feeling conflicting emotions that she might not have felt comfortable sharing with her family. Of course she chose never to reveal all of this explicitly to her children. It was a blight, an imperfection best left forgotten.

Then, in a rather benign detail, I noticed something that hadn't registered before.

Re mum's date of birth I think it's 25.12.42 but cannot find anything with it written on it. Full birth name Elizabeth Julie Winters and yes would have been born in Hawkes Bay (I thought Hastings).

The dots clicked into place for me at that moment – Lizzy's middle name was Julie, the name she gave to her daughter. She didn't pass down a family name to me, but kept it in the hope she would have a legitimate daughter. I was left to assume Cynthia was indeed a completely random, meaningless name.

I was keen to keep the flow of communication going while Julie seemed willing. This was my chance to glean what I could, to find out more truths about my family history, and I didn't want to lose the momentum. I decided to be honest with her, and disclose the possibility that we also shared the same birth father. It felt like a risky move, and she might close up and shut down if she thought I was trying to forge a closer connection with her. I left an out, a safety valve, by telling her about David, too.

Hi Julie,

To be honest, and I'm not sure if Lizzy told you this, but she said there are two men who could be my father. She said one is called David. I wrote to him about 20 years ago and he said he didn't know Lizzy was pregnant which Lizzy said was the case too. He is still alive and lives in Auckland so I hope to have contact with him.

The other man who Lizzy said could be my father was Donald Mackenzie – your father I think? Through Lizzy he had agreed to have contact with me but died before that happened. I'm sorry if that is a bit of a shock but it is what Lizzy told me.

It would be great to see photos of both of them if you are able. I always find it hard to see family likeness but you do look very like Lizzy but I'm not sure if I do?

On the same day that I received my original birth certificate from Oranga Tamariki, Julie replied to me, and included scanned photos of her mother with several 'beaus'. I stared at the photos, each with a few words of context scrawled on the back. The first was not dated but stamped 'Wellington' by the professional photographer. Lizzy wore an evening dress, a cigarette in hand. She was seated beside a handsome man in a tux with a slightly receding hairline who looked older than her.

The other two photos were of Lizzy with men both named David. One was taken in September 1959 at the inter-island wharf with David Thompson, both dressed warmly and David carrying a suitcase in each hand. I assumed they were travelling together to the South Island. On the back of the other, although her writing was hard to read, it said 'David Trikeaux at the nurses Christmas dance, 1960, Wellington Hospital.' I could see Lizzy's likeness to me at the same age in my late teens.

I thought about Lizzy at that time of her life, studying to be a nurse and living in Wellington, away from her unhappy family life, her love of fashion evident in her outfits. Perhaps this was a fresh and hopeful new start for her. She looked pretty and happy and I assumed she seemed to be enjoying her social life with plenty of 'beaus' to go out with. How abruptly it must have come to an end; what a shock it must have been to find herself pregnant. As is the way, the impact on her life was profound while the father, my father, was able to go on with his life unchanged.

In the photo Julie sent me of Lizzy's wedding day, she looked beautiful. Dressed in white with a white veil pulled back from her face, she was in the back seat of the wedding car beside her newly married husband. There was no trace on Lizzy's face of the emotional turmoil she had been through a few short months before.

Recalling my own experience giving birth, and how long it took my body to recover, I was amazed by this photo. Lizzy told me that, 'I came quickly' and that she was young and strong. Still there is no way to hide the sign on a woman's body of pregnancy and birth. Don had known, and must have accepted Lizzy's pre-marital history.

In response to my more sensitive question, Julie replied with a short, simple explanation.

21.12.21

We were told that you were a half sister and that Dad had volunteered to have you as his daughter but mum declined - hard to know really what happened. If you're comfortable, could you let me know what year you were born? I have always assumed you were older than us but I could have that wrong as mum disappeared for a while when we were quite young.

This story echoed Lizzy's tidy version of events that I no longer believed. Instead, I came to understand the choice to adopt was about having a clean start, a white wedding with her husband Don. Refusing his offer to 'raise her child as his own,' as she told me in one of her letters, meant she could wipe her history clean, erase this shameful history and avoid 'the fate' of her parents who I assume conceived Lizzy before they were married. She gave herself a different story, and it began just a few months after my birth.

Here too was confirmation that Lizzy had left the family, that she had disappeared when Julie was young. Though Julie didn't say why, I knew from Lizzy that this must have been the time when she became mentally unwell.

Decisions always make more sense when all the endless human details are uncovered. The compounding pressure, the private grief, all the mounting weight of holding secrets, reinforcing lies. Now it makes sense. She wasn't yet out of her twenties, and she had borne countless traumas. A secret adopted baby, 'I was a ticking time bomb' she had once told me about herself. I hadn't understood before, when she had said it to me.

I wanted to make sense and find the truths that I believe Lizzy tried to obscure, or at least curate a more palatable account of her family and married life. Feeling on the brink of a breakthrough, I pressed for a few more details. I also attached a recent photo of Max and me, hoping she would see the family likeness and perhaps soften her resolve not to include me or Max in her chosen family.

A few days later I slipped, breaking my fibula and injuring my back badly just before Christmas. My painful physical state felt like a mirror of the emotional pain. Was this my body's way of acknowledging what my mind had become so adept at avoiding over all these years? I pushed through the pain to host Christmas at home, then flew to the South Island with my friend Peter. But all that was on my mind was my family history and any further revelations I could extract from Julie.

I was relieved when Julie replied to my pre-Christmas email. Julie conceded that I look like Lizzy, but she wasn't so sure about Max.

Sorry not sure about family likeness - you look like mum but it's always hard when there is a whole other side of your son's family to take into consideration.

I learned in the same email that despite the seemingly happy wedding day, Lizzy's mother was not happy about the marriage. Given what I knew about Lizzy's later 'breakdown,' I wondered what Lizzy's mother had seen and whether she had been right in some way.

I also discovered that Julie and Don were not told about me until they were in their twenties, the mid 1980s. Lizzy first contacted me in 1987, just a few years after the Adult Adoption Information Act 1985. Perhaps Lizzy had known immediately that she would eventually contact me, or maybe she had waited to tell her children until I had responded to that first letter.

> *There was one conversation then, one when I was sick and mum said I should get the consultant to check for Huntington's disease (no I don't have it) and then of course when I saw you at the hospice.*

Lizzy and her husband Donald had kept the secret for more than twenty five years. The weight of carrying an unwanted truth must have been worth the pain. My impulse was to break through the silence and haziness with Julie and lay it all out. *Here's the truth*, I thought, *I'm not going to protect you anymore*. I remembered the time when Lizzy reached the same point in her letters to me when she decided to stop protecting the men who could be my father. Was this the 'courage' she told me was a family trait?

> *Thanks for your notes. I have the case notes from my adoption and they state that Lizzy didn't tell her mother she was pregnant. I was born in 'Motherhood of Man' in Grey Lynn- a charity for unwed mothers so I guess Lizzy took herself away when she found out she was pregnant. That chimes with what I remember her telling me. Lizzy named me Cynthia Winters. I wonder if you know anyone who was important to Lizzy who was named Cynthia? It doesn't seem to be a family name.*
>
> *Can I ask what sickness you had? You said that Lizzy spoke about me when you were sick. I have Addison's disease, a rare autoimmune condition.*
>
> *In one of Lizzy's letters to me she says that while she initially thought David was my father she came to believe it was in fact Don.*

I think she was scared to tell him she thought he was my father but she did tell him not long before he died and he agreed to meet me. As I told you, I was living in Philadelphia at that time and he died before I returned.

I'm really grateful to you for sharing this information with me. I have always been curious about why your brother Don was so determined not to meet me at the hospice and did not want me to come to Lizzy's funeral. I assume it can't be personal as he has never met me and he presumably knew very little about me. Honestly, it is a mystery I would love to have solved. Can you please help me understand?

It was the question I had been burning to ask for sixteen years – and Julie finally gave me the answer.

Re my brother - we are both of the opinion that family is not about blood but rather those that you choose to have as family.. There are a few 'blood relatives' that we have never met for various reasons. So for us it's about those that you are closely linked to etc. My brother's view on this has not changed and I realise that may be harsh but I don't think he will ever want to connect.

Now it was Julie's turn to lay down some truths. It felt brutal. I was not their choice, and the DNA in my blood would not make a difference. Even if I was able to 'prove' that we shared the same father and mother, that we were in fact full siblings, it would not change anything. I was an uncomfortable reality, not a member of the family, and my place was always going to be at arm's length.

But I was still none the wiser as to the true *reason*. Why was I such a complication for Don at Lizzy's funeral? Julie said she was protecting her brother but who was he protecting? His father, even after his death?

As to my discovery about the name Lizzy gave me on my pre-adoption birth certificate, Julie replied:

> *No idea who Cynthia is, never heard that name before. I'm really not at all sure what my dad was told and when — he never discussed it.*
>
> *Re Lizzy's history - completely up to you what you'd like to share.*

I could almost hear the doors slamming. Julie had made it clear that whatever information I found would not convince either of them to embrace me as a sister. Something inside me let go at that point. I was at the end of the line, and the journey from here had to be for me and Max alone.

CHAPTER TWELVE

Are You My Father?

The most unbearable thought of all is that shame was planted in my father's heart and, all the time that he was heroically holding the fragments of his life together, he thought he was hiding from our censure.

Daddy, We Hardly Knew You, Germain Greer

At the same time that Julie and I were emailing back and forth, I rode the wave of my investigation and decided I would try again to contact David. He was the only man possibly still alive who could be my father. Perhaps with time, with distance, he would feel differently about me.

I had promised myself that I would follow the breadcrumb trail of my birth family history. The longer I left it, the fewer crumbs remained, the trail becoming harder to find. Details I felt sure of before started to seem uncertain, others seemed lost to time and memory.

I remembered Lizzy's words when I pressed her over thirty years ago to tell me the names of the men who could be my father. She said, 'You're right. I've decided I'm not going to keep covering for them anymore.' I realised that I had been doing the same thing, feeling it was somehow wrong to intrude and to break the silence and re-contact the only man who might still be alive, David, after twenty years.

If he was the same age as Lizzy when I was conceived, then I calculated that he was at least eighty in 2021. If he was still alive, I thought, I had better take the opportunity. I wouldn't waste this renewed sense of urgency and determination.

With such a unique Greek surname it was easy to find David online. He was alive and he was the owner of a manufacturing company in Auckland. I called the landline and asked in my most breezy way if I could please speak with David. 'He's not here,' said the woman who answered.

'No problem, I'll call him on his mobile if you can give that to me please.' And just like that, I had his number. It was Thursday morning and I decided it was better to call him after work rather than during his busy work day.

I stomped along the beach at Oneroa after dinner, Lizzy's voice speaking indistinguishable words in my head. I was tempted to call my sister Wendy looking for reassurance that I was doing the right thing. But I reasoned with myself, 'I'm not doing anything wrong' and 'If now isn't the right time, when will be?' I knew there was no better time, no right time, I had to act and not allow my fear and the shame and the possible rejection to stop me as it had so many times before. I walked home, went to my study, found the mobile number, and dialled.

David answered. I had my pitch prepared. 'Hi my name is Sue, can we please have a chat?'

'That depends what it's about,' he said, sounding wary.

'You might remember that twenty years ago I wrote to you. I was living in Philadelphia and Lizzy Mackenzie had given me your name as the man who might be my father.' I paused. I sensed his surprise but not a recoil or defence. I told him I would be sixty soon, that I had a thirty year old son. 'I'm sure you can understand, David, that I feel a responsibility to research as much family history as I can and to leave that for my son. That is my work as a parent.'

I acknowledged that things were difficult for him when I first wrote to him, that I remember how much grief he had been going through.

Then, he told me a bit about himself. His second wife had died. He had two children. He hadn't been told about the pregnancy back in the early sixties, but he remembered Lizzy quite clearly.

'She was seeing two of us, you know,' he said.

'Yes I know.'

'At the time Lizzy said she liked his name better than mine,' he remembered. I was silent on the other end of the phone, flinching at the thought of Lizzy saying something so cruel. He carried on quickly, 'Oh well I suppose these things happen. I need to think about what I'm going to tell my children.'

'Yes,' I said, 'but there's so much more acceptance now of these things that happened in the sixties. There have been so many stories on TV and in the newspaper and there's a lot more acceptance in the last twenty years around adoption.'

'I need to think about it.' he said. 'Can you give me a few days to think about this and I will come back to you? If you don't hear back from me in a week then contact me again.'

'Of course, take some time to think about it. David, I'm not looking to find my long-lost father. My motivation is to understand my family history and to be able to pass that on to my son.'

A few days passed, but I didn't hear from David. Following his instructions, I rang him again, but this time I sensed more resistance. He had had time to think about it and he didn't want to have to tell his children or disrupt their family life.

I felt my frustration rising into anger. He asked me how many times I met Lizzy and I told him only twice. 'Why only twice?' he asked, and I could hear the accusation in his voice. Behind his words I heard *Why are you contacting me and making such a big deal if you only saw Lizzy twice? What kind of a daughter are you?* I interpreted his question as a way to let himself off the hook from his responsibility to me – to help me find out the truth about my birth father.

And then he told me, 'She told me to go away, so I did. She told me she preferred the other guy because he had a more masculine name than mine. I don't want to open that up again.' And suddenly it was as if time had collapsed. On the end of the phone wasn't a man in his eighties, but a jilted lover, a hurt young man whose girlfriend rejected him. He was catapulted back, and I could hear the rejection and confusion.

I could imagine Lizzy saying those hurtful words, pushing him away. The deliberate cruelty of telling him his name wasn't 'masculine' enough. But then, she had also told me that David was a good man, the type of man she should have married after all.

'Did she marry Don Mackenzie?' he asked. I told him she did, but their marriage didn't last.

'Why didn't she tell me she was pregnant?' he wondered.

I tried to explain the shame she must have experienced and the difficulty of leaving Wellington to go to Auckland to have her baby in secret. But of course, all I could offer was speculation.

I coached myself – *back off, take it easy, give him time.* 'How about you take some time over Christmas and the holidays to think about it, David. I understand this is a shock. You never know, there might be an opportunity while you're with the family to talk, a natural opening for the conversation.'

'Ok,' he said, 'Leave it with me.'

By the end of the call, I doubted I would hear from him again. I had struck a nerve, an old wound opened. I felt ashamed, too. Why had I only seen Lizzy twice? I could see the pattern of connection and rejection reverberating over time and see that I, too, had been complicit in avoiding what felt too painful, in pushing away Lizzy's need to connect with me just as David was pushing me away.

My doubts were misplaced. On February 7th, 2022, just a few short months after our tense phone call, I was catching a ferry to Auckland to meet David in person.

After a few weeks of space over the holidays, I missed a call from him. Before I even had a chance to dial back, he sent a text:

> *Hi Sue. Happy New Year. Perhaps we can meet for a coffee or a chat sometime if that suits you. David*

It was the message I realised I had been secretly hoping for. I hadn't dared to believe he would get back to me; I couldn't risk another disappointment, another response that would feel like rejection. I replied and we set up a time to meet in the city by the downtown ferry terminal that coming weekend.

On board the Waiheke ferry, I felt a familiar anxiety, the kind that crops up just before going on a blind date when you're wondering if you'll like each other or have anything in common. I was trying to keep my emotions in check, not wanting to expect anything, not wanting to hope for too much. But at my core, I guessed he was going to be open with me, willing to share what he knew.

Dressed deliberately casually in shorts and a t-shirt, I walked out of the ferry terminal onto Quay Street. I could see a man I immediately assumed was David waiting outside our agreed meeting place. He was easy to spot. A slender, distinguished looking older man with straight silver hair, well-dressed, and leaning lightly on a wooden cane on his right side. The Omicron outbreak was in full force, so my face was covered in a mask. I tried to show I was smiling as I approached him.

He was also wearing a mask but his eyes peered over in a welcoming openness that put me at ease. The tension I was holding inside of me released; I felt safe with him.

The coffee shop where we had planned on meeting was closed on Sunday so we went inside the Commercial Bay shopping centre, making small talk on the way. Near the escalator we found a place where we could grab a couple of takeaway coffees. I accepted his offer to pay and we walked through to sit on the public overbridge between Commercial Bay and the Downtown car park, looking out towards the water and the ferry terminal.

It was a gentle moment. We had nothing but space and time to chat. I thanked him for being willing to meet with me, and I meant it. I could feel the warmth of his presence, an intangible familial connection. There was a sense that we shared history, but without shared memory we were only just starting to write our relationship.

He told me about his children; his daughter Natalie, an accountant, and his son Christopher, a manager in Wellington. He showed me a photo with his children and grandchildren, a 'typical' smiling Kiwi family probably taken at Matarangi where he said they regularly spent their summer holidays at their beach house.

He asked if I had been able to find out any more information about Lizzy. I told him about her father leaving the family after he was physically and mentally damaged from the War and then how she also had become mentally unwell, eventually leaving her children and her husband and some time after that coming to find me.

I told David again that I didn't know if he was my father. Lizzy, at least at one point, had been '98 percent certain' that he was, but then later in her life seemed equally certain that my father was Donald, the man that she married.

We talked about how strange it was to be meeting in this way, to make a connection and share the rough outline of our lives with each other, if we were to find out that in fact we weren't related at all. Despite the strangeness though, it was an easy conversation; I liked him. I felt a hope rising in me that he was my birth father, that this kind, intelligent eighty-six-year-old man in good mental and physical health was my father and that his genetic history would somehow neutralise the worst aspects of my maternal genes. I had been feeling a mounting sense of horror at the genetic cocktail I had inherited from my birth mother's side of the family.

David said he had Greek heritage. Eventually his ancestors made their way to Wellington, New Zealand, where there was a small community of Greeks. David was fourteen at the time. He spoke very little English, and his parents almost none. They had left Europe with nothing, and then completely rebuilt their lives in New Zealand. His father was well-educated but his limited English made it difficult in a new country.

David then told me how his first wife was killed in a car accident. They were hit by a van crossing the centre line. His wife was killed instantly, and David and both of his children were seriously injured.

David married again and his second wife died of cancer. He was now living in a retirement village in Auckland and said he didn't think he would marry again. I quietly marvelled at his clarity of mind and openness which I found surprising in a man of his age. I told him, 'I hope you are my birth father.'

There was a tentative and gentle familiarity between us, like two people who have been accidentally caught up in the same difficult life circumstance bringing with it some kind of obligation and a connection over and above what would be expected in a first meeting. After about forty five minutes, it felt like time to end the meeting. I said, 'I don't know how to do this because what if I find out we're not related?'

I told him I was going to do a DNA test through Google and I would let him know the results. He offered to do one too but I thanked him and said that shouldn't be necessary. As far as I know, Lizzy's family were English and Irish so if there was any evidence of Greek ancestry that would likely tell us that he was my father.

We thanked each other for the meeting. He told me his son and daughter were happy for us to meet and wanted to know from him how it went. I asked if I could reach out to his daughter Natalie and he was happy for me to do that.

Going home on the ferry, I couldn't help but compare this meeting with the distant coolness I had experienced from Lizzy's children. Julie and Don, who I knew to be at least my half brother and sister, had been so fearful of my existence, not wanting any kind of relationship or acknowledgement of our familial connection. In contrast, here was David, who didn't even know if he was my birth father, and his two adult children who were willing to connect with me and to extend his kindness even before we had confirmed any kind of genetic relation.

I felt joy and gratitude and a sense of relief. If he was my father, I believed it would bring me a feeling of calm, belonging. Perhaps we could even develop a relationship, tie our families together.

I knew I wanted Max to meet him if he was my birth father, for Max to meet someone from my birth family, to have something good to give him along with the hard history of Lizzy's family, something that would bring a sense of pride and reassurance. Here was a family history I could connect with and offer to Max, reuniting him with long lost relatives.

Maybe it was also a hope or affirmation that I wasn't built from something entirely broken. Lizzy was anxious to assure me of the strengths and positive qualities in her family, but I had been finding it hard to acknowledge them. It seemed easier to meet and to like this man, to recognise his courage and generosity in finally being willing to meet me and to help me find answers.

I left my meeting with David carrying something I didn't have before: hope. Hope that I could look into the eyes of a man I actually liked and know he was my father and that he liked me too.

Like a small treasure hidden in my pocket, I held onto this hope stone, this thing that might or could be an answer that would help me make sense of my birth history. That I could belong to this kind, resilient family who were just as curious about me as I was about them. How extraordinary, I thought, if I had found my birth father, aged eighty-six, in the middle of a global pandemic, and my image reflected in his eyes.

He also said that his children would like to meet me. After so many years of being shut out of Lizzy's family, it was a strange feeling to be welcomed warmly by David and his children. As soon as I got home I sent a message to his eldest daughter Natalie via LinkedIn asking to connect.

Hi Natalie- Thxs for accepting my request. Lovely to meet your father this morning.

She responded right away.
Hi Sue. Great to connect. Dad said it was lovely to meet you too.

Lovely? It was lovely to meet me? They were pleasantries, and yet this word was so much more than that. I realised this was the first time in any written communication that I had someone on this search for my birth family history who referred to my existence as *lovely*. Tolerated, resented, angry, ignored – these were the words expected of a child unchosen. 'Lovely' was just about the kindest thing Natalie could have said in her reply.

While we worked to find a time to meet in our busy calendars I decided to take a DNA test through 23andMe. I wanted to know for sure, to validate that small treasure of hope. David had offered at our meeting to take a test, a big shift from twenty years ago when I asked if he would be willing to take a DNA test to help me confirm my paternity. I could have said yes but I wanted to do it as quickly and simply as possible and not ask that of him.

So I spat into a plastic tube. All I needed was a DNA result from 23andMe to say, 'Yes, you are Greek.' Just a couple weeks later, I had my results. I clicked open the email, signed into the account, and there it was:

100% European
98.5% Northwestern European
92.1% British & Irish
2.7% French & German
2.7% Scandinavian
1% Broadly Northwestern European

No sign of Greek blood. A clear answer, one of only a few throughout the years. But not the answer I wanted.

My first instinct was to delete it or leave it unsaved in my emails, to discard it. Opening the box, closing it again tighter than before. David was not my father. Odds were that my Irish blood was the product of Don, the man who once said he'd shoot Lizzy if he ever found out 'that baby' was his. And if this was true – of course it probably was – then I was a full sibling to Julie and Don Jnr.

I called David to tell him. The details, even these recent ones, curl and fray at their edges. He told me that he was disappointed by the results, that he would have been delighted to have been my father.

Despite the DNA results I decided to still go ahead and meet Natalie. I had been in isolation with my housemate with COVID, then away for ANZAC weekend and Easter break.

We finally found a time to meet in June, at a cafe in the Auckland CBD, not far from where I met David. It was a workday, and we were both dressed for the office. From a distance, we would have appeared to be two professional women meeting to discuss business. Natalie, an accountant; myself, a leadership coach and director. But very quickly, we established a sense of familiarity with one another. She was curious to know my story, and asked me about my birth mother, my history and the path that led to her father. At times, I became tearful, and she was there, compassionate, thoughtful, taking in my story with a quiet assurance.

It was as though she saw all that I had wanted and been denied from my birth family, and wanted, in some small way, to repair the damage with her acceptance of me. Where Lizzy's family reluctantly relinquished each detail and carefully stepped around the stains of the family tapestry, Natalie listened and shared some of her family history and the tragedy they had experienced when her mother was killed in the car accident.

I wondered why she had decided to be so generous with her time and her stories and her kindness towards me, despite knowing that we might not share a drop of blood. Even before we met, I felt a connection too, a sense that we could offer one another something meaningful, even if only through our stories. I also think she knew how much I had impacted her father. She had this sense of fearlessness, that she wasn't afraid or ashamed of what the connection with me might say about her father and his past. She didn't want to run away, or hide her past, or protect her family from me.

Straight after our meeting Natalie messaged me again via LinkedIn.

Hi Sue. Really good to meet you today. My contact details below so we can keep in touch! Take Care, N.

We exchanged emails, and left the door wide open to one day walk through again and greet one another as friends.

On February 8th, 2024, Natalie reached out to me again.

Hi Sue. I hope you're well. Would it suit for me to give you a quick call? Thanks, Natalie X

I knew the moment I got the message. I called her straight away and she told me that David had died just before Christmas from pneumonia, surrounded by his family in a hospital bed. She cried on the phone as she told me.

Almost exactly twenty years after Lizzy's death, I quietly acknowledged the passing of a kind man who was willing to embrace me as a daughter. Another funeral I was not invited to, but this time I understood why. While David had bravely acknowledged me to his children, he told me he felt ashamed of the relationship with Lizzy that happened before he met his wife. Coming from a Greek Orthodox family, even more than sixty years later, that was not something he wanted his friends and wider family to know.

I was reminded of my phone call with David two years before this. His heartbreak over Lizzy, the shame she placed on him for a name that wasn't 'masculine' enough. His flawless Kiwi accent despite moving to New Zealand without knowing English at fourteen suggests he would have worked very hard very quickly to assimilate. But still she rejected his background, his culture, and she left without ever telling him she was pregnant. I realised how startling it would have been for him, sixty years later, to be confronted by a woman who had Lizzy's fine, straight hair and slender face, telling him that he might have another daughter.

I felt lucky to have had the privilege of meeting him, of his acceptance, no matter what my DNA test showed in the end. I hoped that acknowledging and respecting him had helped in some way to heal the wounds Lizzy opened before I was born.

Not long after, I asked Natalie if we could meet once again. I wanted to express my condolences, and make it clear how appreciative I was of her father. I took a small bunch of white flowers, pretty but simple. She was genuinely touched by the gesture. We talked more openly this time about her family and the health challenges many of them have faced. I admired her calmness and acceptance of all that she had been through.

Her brother had a medical incident while he was on a call with Natalie and David about a year ago. They were there to support him after he was discharged from hospital. But not long after, he had another more serious incident and fell to the floor. Natalie immediately began CPR while David ran next door to get help and call the ambulance. The doctors said he was lucky to survive and that Natalie had literally saved his life.

The doctors suggested Natalie also get checked, so she had a scan. She ended up having to undergo extensive treatment. In a twelve month period her brother had almost died, she was experiencing a significant medical event, and her father died. There was no drama in the telling, just a quiet narrative of the facts and tears from both of us.

I realised this had all happened before we first met but she hadn't told me. Another sign of her generosity. Holding back this story so she could give me her full attention and the story of my search for my birth family history.

Natalie didn't have any reason to open herself to me, to let me in as you'd allow a close friend or a long lost family member. I suppose I didn't have any reason to follow up with her either. But we both chose to lay this ground before us. Another thread, woven consciously from one woman to another, from one family of Greek origin with a deemed-unacceptable surname to another family of British-Irish origin with a name erased. The only connection was that her father had a relationship with my mother sixty-one years ago.

CHAPTER THIRTEEN

He Punga Aroha
The Anchor of Love

We fell.
Yet we were loved and we were lifted.
We froze.
Yet we were loved and we are warm.
We broke apart.
Yet we are here and we are whole.

Erebus Voices, Bill Manhire

August 2024

I didn't want to accept the finality of my first DNA results. Despite the '98% English and Irish' test, my heart told me there was more to the story. Perhaps a minor strand of Greek heritage was hidden somewhere in my DNA, waiting to be uncovered. I had read that this was possible, that daughters may not show much of the DNA of their fathers.

I felt as if I was on the verge of a discovery that would pull all the pieces of the puzzle together. That if I could only find the right link, the right test, I would find the closure I was now willing to admit to myself that I wanted. I wanted to be related to David and Natalie and Christopher. I wanted to be Greek. I wanted to believe that Lizzy was telling the truth right from the beginning in her first version of my conception and birth story.

The 23andMe results from last year told a story that I wasn't ready to accept. Christopher was the one last chance to find out once and for all who my father was.

Natalie said that Christopher was keen to see me even though at that time it seemed certain that we weren't related. He was in Auckland over a long weekend and we agreed to meet in the city with Natalie.

Once again, I found myself nervous with anticipation in a crowded central city cafe, facing the door so I could see the siblings as they came through the door. I recognized Natalie right away. Beside her, a tall man, younger than us, who instantly reminded me of his father. Christopher had the same friendly curves in his smile and the same dark eyes. He was a handsome man – no doubt like his father David when Lizzy met him in Wellington over sixty years ago.

I felt a wash of uncertainty – knowing, logically, that he likely wasn't my true brother – splashing against one of hope – the instant familiarity I felt as he reached out to shake my hand and then to hug each other.

He was quieter than his sister, but Natalie's easy nature smoothed the way as we began to talk. I asked where he lived and we traded memories of familiar Wellington landmarks. We had traversed the same streets, ate at the same restaurants, two almost-siblings never crossing paths. He was a considered man, intelligent in his words. His gentle spirit put me at ease, and I found myself talking freely.

I shared a short version of my story. All the stones I had gathered and discovered over the last thirty-odd years. It was hard to put into words the respect I felt for their father and the deep gratitude I had that their family had been so accepting and welcoming. This was in stark contrast to the way my other siblings, at least half related to me, had treated me.

Natalie and Christopher owed me nothing. The DNA results showed no Greek ancestry, yet still they were here, willing to walk alongside me as I dared to hope for a different answer. 'The research I've done shows that if someone from my birth father's family line tested alongside me, I would know for sure,' I explained.

I asked Christopher if he would be willing to do a DNA test – an echo of the same question I'd asked his father when I first had connected with him. But unlike David, who had first been so hesitant to accept a final answer, Christopher was more than willing. Neither he or Natalie had ever taken an ancestry test before, and he was curious. We agreed to use a different platform this time – ancestry.com – and share our results when the time came.

So many years, so many rejections, and finally, I would have something tangible. The final bend in the road before revealing my family history, my identity, laid out before me.

We took a photo: the three of us grinning together, surrounded by the clinks of china and the chatter of strangers enjoying their public holiday. I poured over it afterwards, looking for clues that would point to shared genetics. 'Can you see the family likeness?' I would ask my Max, my sister Wendy, my friends.

I wanted to see a pattern of recognition. A precursor to the results I was vying for. But their answers were polarising. Some instantly saw a connection; others looked at me with scepticism in their eyes as they admitted to seeing nothing more than friends enjoying coffee.

A couple of weeks later, in the middle of June, after I had sent off my sample to ancestry.com, I went to Hot Water Beach to meet with my editor, Elsa, and review the manuscript. We read back the chapter of when I first met Natalie and received the first round of DNA results. It wasn't an easy chapter to write, and I felt deflated as I tried to be realistic about all the evidence we had put together for the book.

But maybe, just maybe, there was something else we had missed. There was a tiny light of hope that refused to extinguish inside me. Natalie and Christopher and David had all seemed so familiar to me. I had to know for sure before I could move on.

After a long day of writing and editing, I walked down to the famous Coromandel beach to clear my head. With my hands, I dug into the hot sand, searching for the ancient water to flood my shallow pool. I felt the heat and the compressed CO_2 rise from the deep earth, allowing it to soak into my skin as I sat looking out at the white breaking waves of the vast

Pacific Ocean. There in the winter sunshine I imagined visiting Greece and walking through its warm Mediterranean waters, what it would feel like to know I was walking on my own ancestral land.

That night, I went to bed early as I often do when I'm away from home. But I couldn't seem to find sleep, and it was after midnight before I finally drifted off. At 4am, I woke up quite suddenly and could see the bright light of the full moon shining around the edges of the curtains.

With stark clarity, Cynthia came into my mind. The name Lizzy gave me at birth, the first etching of my existence on paper. As though guided by some kind of force, I felt compelled to search for the origin of the name. In all my research, I suddenly realised that I had never thought to do that before. A quick Google on my phone revealed that Cynthia was a Greek name meaning 'moon goddess.' There is a Mt Cynthus on Delos Island, supposedly the birthplace of the goddess Artemis. Cynthia is the moon personified, 'a creative, and a visionary.' Could Lizzy have given me this name knowing it was of Greek origin, as a signifier of my own Greek heritage?

This new information jolted me fully awake. I felt as if Cynthia herself had woken me up. Forgotten, discarded, and starved of love, of recognition – she had finally grown loud enough to make her presence known. To finally be seen and understood and accepted, not just as some orphaned newborn baby but as a living soul within me.

I stood up, pulled back the curtains and looked into the brightness of the full moon, allowing the blue light to touch my skin and soak into me. It was then that I finally embraced her, the child Cynthia, and told her she was always welcome here in my life and that I would protect her from now on.

The next morning, with Cynthia at the top of my mind, I began to question once again why Lizzy had given me this name. It seemed too much of a coincidence that Lizzy would have chosen a Greek name for her baby when she believed my father to be Greek. But at the same time, there had been so many accidental connections and dualities that I couldn't allow myself to fully believe this was truly a sign of my heritage.

It would be months before I would get my ancestry results back so I messaged Christopher to find out if Cynthia was perhaps a family name on his father's side, perhaps a relative David would have mentioned to Lizzy in the time they knew each other.

When Christopher replied saying he didn't know anyone in the family called Cynthia, I was left to wonder once again. I hoped that Lizzy had chosen the name knowing its origins, that perhaps it was her homage to the father I would never know.

In early August, Christopher received his results. 17 percent Greek, then a mix of other Germanic and British heritage. No surprises there.

It was only a few days later that I received my own:

46% England and Northwestern Europe
45% Scotland
5% Ireland
4% Norway

There it was. Nothing from Greece. Nothing to indicate any relation whatsoever. I felt my heart sink. This was the end of the trail.

But when I looked closer at the results online, I could see that I had matched with a close relative, a first cousin with the surname Mackenzie. If this was true, it would be the indisputable proof that I was indeed the daughter of Don Mackenzie. And therefore, Julie and Don Junior were my full siblings.

I messaged Eleanor, my supposed first cousin, immediately.

Hi Eleanor - reaching out as it looks like we are first cousins. Are you related to Donald Mackenzie from Wellington – in his late 50s and Donald Mackenzie (senior) his father who has now died? Hope to hear from you. Thanks, Sue

I had become so accustomed to endless waiting, to gruelling days of breadcrumb answers that it took me by surprise when I received a rapid, friendly reply from my cousin.

Hi Sue. I sure am. Donald Mackenzie from Wellington is my cousin, and his father was Uncle Donald. Uncle Donald was born in 1935 and died in 2000. Who are your parents and grandparents?

I replied with a brief explanation and my contact details.

Eleanor called me immediately. The self-proclaimed 'family historian,' she was confused that she couldn't locate me on her family tree. When I told her why, I could almost feel her heart rate pick up on the other side of the phone in excitement. Eleanor was an untapped vessel of family stories and explanations, a total contrast to the Mackenzie family I had come to expect.

When I asked about Lizzy and Don, she painted me a colourful portrait of her experience growing up as their niece. Lizzy was the 'posh' aunt, always wearing fashionable clothing and turning up to their house driving a Jaguar. The sense I got was that to Eleanor, Lizzy gave off the air of someone a little too good for the family she had married into. Eleanor had no idea about the biggest family secret of all – me.

Don, Eleanor told me, was a private man. Even when Lizzy was committed to the psychiatric unit, he never reached out to his siblings or the rest of the family for support. He raised his children on his own, kept up with his work, and otherwise stayed much to himself. Eleanor's memories of visiting him in the big two storied house in Paekākāriki were of walking into a dark, quiet room with Don sitting in an old armchair, smoke writhing around him in thick tendrils, a glass of whiskey seated beside him. The image made me shudder.

She told me about her grandmother – my grandmother – Mary, born in Australia, the eldest of ten children. And the spinster sister of the family. Various other characters, great-aunts and second cousins I had never come across before.

It wasn't a close family. But Eleanor was determined to learn more about their roots. When I spoke to her, she had a trip booked to Ireland to try to uncover more details about their ancestry. We agreed to stay in touch and perhaps get together in Wellington when she returned from Ireland.

Strangely, however, I didn't feel an edge of anticipation as I ended our call. That itch for more information, more answers, more connections was fading, like a plug in the sink had been pulled and all my desire drained out.

I had more answers than ever before, more finality and assurance, and even a birth relative excited to talk with me. It was everything I had been looking for. Yet, I felt a sense of indifference overlaid by, I reluctantly admitted to myself, disappointment. This wasn't how it was supposed to happen. I felt my familiar response of shrugging off and detaching from my birth family, a form of protection from so many failed attempts at connection.

To this day, I haven't told my birth brother and sister the results yet. They've made their view clear: we choose our family, and we don't choose you. I assume that a confirmation of our genetics would have no impact. When I first heard Don and then later Julie explain their disinterest in building a connection with me, it felt like a razor's edge. It was personal, and it was hurtful. But now, I understand. Now that the choice feels like it is mine to make, I can accept theirs.

I will turn sixty-two in just a few weeks, the age my birth mother was when her life ended. She passed onto me many half-finished stories and incomplete details and more questions than answers. But she also gave me a wonderful gift – the start of a journey I would have never begun on my own. Lizzy took the first step in finally breaking free of the rejection, the compounded hurt and fear that started long before my life and back into generations of alcoholism and broken families and lives spent in the shadow of shame. I realise now that erasure takes time to be undone, for what was hidden to be revealed. It takes love to bring it back to life only to lay it back again to rest in peace. It was my role to finish the work she had started.

I remember when Lizzy decided to open up to me about my birth father, to 'stop protecting' them. Her trepidation as she cracked open the gate she had held for thirty years. Near the end of her life she told me she had thought about it again and realised she was '98 percent certain' Don was my father. This was the truth, at the end of the day. She would die not knowing for sure, but having given me the clues I needed to find the answers.

When I pulled out the white box three years ago, I wasn't looking for a new family. I wanted to understand, to know, to see everything that I was and that I am. With each new stone I collected, I knew I would have to throw many back into the riverbed, otherwise the weight of my pockets would pull me down. Now, I have written my story. And with the words, I've revealed and released the shame and the secrets that kept us all hidden and trapped for so long.

I now know my whakapapa, where I am from. I have come to accept and respect Lizzy, my birth mother. Found my birth father, Don, and my full sister and brother and connected with a first cousin on my father's side. I learned my birth name and the story of my days before adoption. Found a beautiful Greek family that I am connected with only by a short relationship between our parents over sixty years ago. And most importantly, I found Cynthia, who had been with me all this time. Watchful, afraid, distrustful. She had tried so hard to protect me, to keep me safe the only way she knew how – by keeping others away, to abandon before being abandoned again. Now I see you, Cynthia. I hold you in my arms, and I promise to love you and care for you.

Together, we are complete and we are *tau*, at peace.

Tomorrow, I will call my son and do my best for him as he continues his journey. I will think of my tuākana, my older sister Wendy and the unconditional love she gives me. I will be gracious to my birth and non-birth siblings, however unfamiliar or untethered our lives might be. And I will carry Cynthia close, and never let her be alone again.

Kua mutu, it has finished.

ACKNOWLEDGEMENTS

My first acknowledgement goes to my family, to Mum and Dad, Wendy, Max and Jem, and my grandson Xavier. I wrote this for you and with you in my heart. Thank you for being my family. Thanks to my birth mother 'Lizzie' and Cynthia who have been there since the beginning. Thanks to my wider whānau: Jude and Diana, who have been my close friends for the whole journey of connection with my birth history. Thanks to Peter, Maikara, Tim, Tess and my Waiheke whānau for listening, support and belonging. Thanks to my literary mentor, Mike Johnson, who told me I could write like this. Thanks to my writing companions Emily and Teresa and the Quaker Friend's House and Hot Water beach for spaces to write. Thanks to the team at Lasavia Publishing for your expertise in publishing this book so it can be shared. Finally and importantly, thanks to Elsa Klein, my writing collaborator and editor. I will be forever grateful that you answered my call for help, for your wisdom and insights and your ability to draw the story from me and help me craft something for others to read.

Ngā mihi nui ki a koutou.

ABOUT THE AUTHOR

Sue lives on Waiheke Island where she shares her home with women of many ages and cultures. A former academic, life-long researcher, and leader, she now dedicates her work to supporting women leaders, advocating for social housing, and contributing to a more equitable and inclusive Aotearoa. This memoir is her first personal writing project.

www.ingramcontent.com/pod-product-compliance
Lightning Source LLC
Chambersburg PA
CBHW021207130626
46554CB00005B/2026